CYPRUS

The island of Aphrodite

1999

Text: MARY ANASTASIOU
Text edited by: DAPHNE CHRISTOU
Translation: DAVID HARDY
Design: EVI DAMIRI

Colour separations - printing: M. TOUBIS GRAPHIC ARTS S.A.

Exclusive distributor in Cyprus: IOANNOU & GEORGIOU, Tel: (02) 890491, Fax: (02) 490106, Nicosia

We wish to thank the **Press and Information Office of the Rebublic of Cyprus** for the valuable material
and photographs it made available to us.
We also extend our thanks to the photographer **Mr. Stelios Yasemidis** and to the biologist
and ecological expert **Mr. Gr. Tsounis**, who made a particularly valuable contribution to the publication of this book.

*"Would that I could visit Cyprus,
the island of Aphrodite,
where the enchanting cupids
sport with mortals..."*

Euripides, *«Bacchae»*

CONTENTS

CONTENTS

1 CYPRUS

Cyprus, the beautiful island of Aphrodite, emerged from the crystal-clear waters of the south-east Mediterranean. To it, according to tradition, "the breath of Zephyr carried the goddess of love on the white foam, amidst the sounding sea."

The presence of the goddess of beauty is still reflected everywhere on the island: in the gardens with their intoxicating scent of lemon-blossom and jasmine, the plains with their countless almond-trees, silvery-green olives, and abundant apple- and cherry-trees, the pine forests and ravines, and the lacy, indented coasts with their golden beaches. The people, too, at harmony with the landscape, are genuine and optimistic, endowed by nature with beauty of spirit and a determination to struggle with the "elements" of their lives and emerge victorious. They greet you with their warmest smile and generously offer you their all.

Ever since ancient times, Cyprus has had many names, stressing its natural beauty: Aeria, Galenia, Euploia, Makaria, Kyprida Ourania, Perikalle, and Aphrodisia, as well as Island of Love.

The history of Cyprus is so long that it is difficult to encapsulate it in a brief account. Its strategic position at the cross-roads of three continents (Europe, Asia, and Africa), and its rich crops and mines determined its tumultuous historical destiny from very ancient times. Cyprus became — and is still today — an apple of strife.

"Leda and the Swan".
Mosaic from the "House of Aion".

The island of Aphrodite

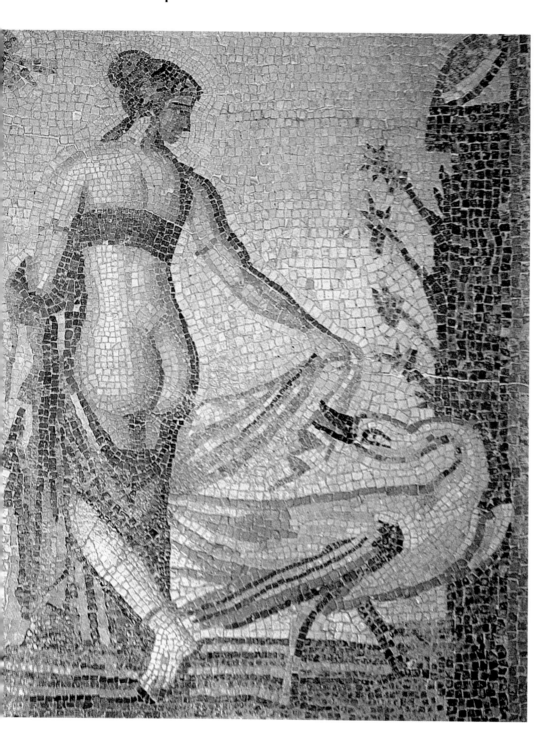

During the long history of the island, many conquers have set foot on its soil (Phoenicians, Assyrians, Egyptians, Persians, Franks, Venetians, Ottoman Turks, and British). Amazingly, although all these foreign peoples have left indelible traces on the personality of the Cyprus countryside, they did not succeed in corrupting the Greek character and culture of its inhabitants.

Cyprus itself is a distinctive historical and ethnographic museum, in which visitors can travel through time and admire a unique cultural mosaic composed of prehistoric settlements, ancient Greek temples, Byzantine churches, with their wonderful mosaics and wall-paintings, Crusader castles, Gothic churches, Venetian forts, Turkish mosques, and modern British roads. Faced with all this, visitors will be dazzled and will undoubtedly try in their imagination to relive those remote periods and stand alongside Alexander the Great, Cicero, St. Paul, Richard the Lionheart, and all the others who trod the same places.

The island also has a superb climate and excellent tourist infrastructure. Throughout the entire year, thousands of visitors flock here from all parts of the world, to enjoy the beauty of a land that is eager to unfold its secrets to those who like to search out ancient traditions and civilisations.

1. *The Castle of Paphos.*
2. *The church of Ayia Kyriaki in the centre of Paphos.*
3. *Neolithic settlement at Chirokitia.*
4. *Ancient theatre at Paphos.*

NATURE

Location - Morphology - Geology - Climate
Topography - Flora - Fauna

Location - Morphology

Cyprus lies at the south-east end of the Mediterranean, of which it is the third largest island after Sicily and Sardinia. The easternmost of the Mediterranean islands, it is flanked by Asia, Europe and Africa, being 100 km. west of Syria, 75 km. south of Turkey, 380 km. north of Egypt, and 270 km. east of Kastel-

Visitors are captivated by the natural environment of Cyprus.

lorizo, the south-eastern extremity of Greece. Cyprus covers an area of 9,251 square km.; it is 225 km. long (from its easternmost to its westernmost tip), 94 km. wide at its widest point, and has 853 km. of coastline. The population of the island is about 700,000, and it is divided into 6 provinces: Nicosia, Limassol, Larnaca, Paphos, Famagusta and Kyrenia. With the exception of a small part of Famagusta, the last two provinces have been occupied by Turkish forces since the summer of 1974, together with part of the province of Nicosia. The capital of the island is Nicosia, which has a population of about 177,000. Other important towns in the free areas include the capitals of the other provinces, which have the same names as the provinces them-

selves: Limassol has 140,000 inhabitants, Larnaca 43,600, and Paphos 32,500. The temporary capital of the unoccupied area of the province of Famagusta is Paralimni, which has 7,700 inhabitants. Cyprus as a whole cannot be described as a mountainous land, but a large part of it is nevertheless covered with mountains and the greater parts of the provinces of Limassol, Paphos and Kyrenia are mountainous. There are two ranges on Cyprus: Pentadaktylos (1023 m) and Troodos, the highest peak of which is Olympos (or Chionistra), at 1951 m. These ranges are separated by the plain of Mesaoria, and there is a narrow peninsula called Karpasia in the east of the island.

The geophysical map of Cyprus is marked with the courses of a large number of rivers. In fact, these are torrents that only carry water in the winter months and dry up in the summer. These little rivers have carved out deep, attractive valleys, which give the countryside of Cyprus its own particular flavour. The most important of them are the Pedieos (Pidias), the Ezousas, the Diarizos, the Xeros, the Kourris and the Yalias.

The island has several springs. There are two famous springs in the province of Kyrenia, both called Kephalovryso, one near the village of Kythrea and the other near Lapithos. Other well-known mineral, healing springs are to be found near the Ayios Chrysostomos Monastery, near Buffavento (Kyrenia), and at the village of Kalopanayiotis in the Troodos range, and there are others of lesser importance. The only lakes on Cyprus are the salt-lakes of Larnaca and Limassol.

1. The copper mine at Skouriotissa.
2. One of the attractive springs of Cyprus.

Geology

In the Eocene era, the area occupied by Cyprus was probably connected with other areas of dry land in the neighbouring continents. At some point in time, however, this area was submerged beneath the sea, and the original surface was buried beneath many thousands of feet of marine sediments, at a great depth beneath sea level.

This subsidence continued throughout the entire Holocene and the greater part of the Miocene eras, after which volcanic activity reversed the trend, resulting in the land re-emerging from the sea and forming the Troodos range. Troodos was an island of volcanic rock and probably formed the kernel of the later island. Eleven million years later, towards the end of the Miocene era, volcanic activity led to great pressure that resulted in the formation of the Kyrenia range of Pentadaktylos. The plain of Mesaoria remained submerged beneath the sea, emerging much later during the Pleistocene era. The turbulent geological history of the island accounts for its wide variety of rocks. Volcanic, igneous, and sedimentary rocks, limestones of different colours and compositions, are all to be found close together on the surface of the island, giving the Cypriot landscape a continually changing appearance.

Climate

Cyprus enjoys a Mediterranean climate, one of the mildest in Europe, with average sunshine of 74 % and an average annual temperature of 19°C. Summers are hot and humid. They usually begin in the middle of May and end in the middle of October. The hottest months are July and August, with average temperatures of 32°C. Winters are mild and last from November to the end of February. The coldest months are January and February with average temperatures of 14°C.
In recent years, the average rainfall in Cyprus has been 503 mm. The greatest rainfall is to be found in the western areas and the mountainous and semi-mountainous regions. Snow is a very rare phenomenon in the plains, though it snows quite frequently on the higher peaks of Troodos, especially in the months of January and February. Temperatures vary from region to region, ranging from 30°C in the mountain villages to in excess of 30°C in the plains and central areas.

The landscape of Cyrpus is of great interest at all seasons of the year.

Topography

Topographically, the island may be divided into five regions.

First region: The mountain range of Kyrenia or Pentadaktylos, which rises in the north of the island like a protective wall facing the central plain. Geologically, this consists of solid limestones, and it stretches for over 160 km. from the cape of Apostolos Andreas. The west part of it is known as the Kyrenia mountains, and the east as Karpasia. The highest peak in this range is Kyparissovouno, which is 1023 m. high.

Second region: The Troodos complex, composed mainly of serpentine. The Troodos range, which covers almost the whole of west Cyprus, is formed of volcanic rocks, with sheer slopes, and deep, narrow valleys; it also has some copper, asbestos and chromium mines. The highest peak is Olympos, which is 1951 m. high. Other peaks include Madara (1612 m), Papoutsa (1554 m), Tripylos (1362 m), Kykkos (1318 m), Stavropefkos (1234 m), and two lower peaks, Macheras and Stavrovouni. The sources of all the rivers of Cyprus of any note are to be found in the Troodos range, and the area is accordingly of enormous importance for the water-supplies of the island. Many of the dams of Cyprus are to be found in this region.

Third region: The hilly region around Troodos and to the south of the Kyrenia range is characterised mainly by round, almost bare, white hills consisting of soft, white, chalky earth. These areas are not irrigated, and the main crop cultivated in them is the vine.

Fourth region: The central plain of Cyprus, the Mesaoria, or Mesarka, extends between the two parallel mountain ranges of Pentadaktylos and Troodos. It is a low, elongated, alluvial, highly fertile plain with low hills.

The plain is about 90 km. long from the bay of Morphou to the bay of Famagusta, and it ranges in width from 16 to 23 km. The south-east end of it is called Kokkinochoria ("red villages"), because the soil here has a reddish colour.

Fifth region: in the north is a narrow coastal zone with an intricately indented coastline, known as the plain of Kyrenia. The plain of Larnaca in the south is a low, alluvial plain. Its most significant feature is the salt-lake of Larnaca, which in winter forms an ideal wetland for a large number of migratory birds, though it dries up in the summer.

Still in the south, the plain of Limassol occupies the Akrotiri peninsula, extending as far as Pissouri and Avdimou in the west, and there are also some small areas of it to the east of Amathus. The most important geological feature here is the lake of Akrotiri. In recent geological times there was an island between the capes of Zevgari and Gata. The alluvial material steadily deposited at the mouth of the rivers Garillis and Kourris, at the east and west of the island respectively, led to its unification with the main island, creating the salt-lake in between. Other coastal plains include those of Paphos and of Chrysochou. The former is a narrow strip stretching from Petra tou Romiou to the settlement of Ayios Yeoryios Peyias. The latter lies to the east and west of the town of Chrysochou and includes part of the narrow valley of Chrysochou to the south of the town.

CYPRUS

SCALE: 1:680,000

Motorway		Church
Metalled road		Monastery
Unmetalled road		Castle
Dirt road		Archaeological site
Motorway exit		Lighthouse
Distance in km		Organised beach
Area occupied by Turkish forces		Water sports
British military Bases		Anchorage
Airport		Campsite
		Nature trails

Flora

Cyprus, lying at the cross-roads between three continents, enjoys climatic conditions suitable for the evolution of many plants and animals.

In ancient times Cyprus was covered with thick forests, concealing the mountains and plains. Nowadays, the forests are confined to the Pentadaktylos and Troodos ranges and the hilly areas around them. The trees mainly found are the Aleppo pine, cypress, the cedar, the poplar, the plane-tree and others.

In addition to the familiar vegetation found in the Mediterranean, there are 127 species of plant native to the island, more than half of them in the Troodos range.

Troodos has a distinctive flora, as a result of its geological composition and the special ecological conditions created by the great heights above sea level, the rainfall and the temperatures. It is home to many of the indigenous species of Cyprus that are not found in other parts of the island.

A rare and rich variety of shrubs and flowers is also to be found on the island, and twenty of them have been proposed for inclusion in the list of strictly protected species of European flora. Typical such species are wild orchids and cyclamen. In springtime, Cyprus has a rare beauty, with over 300 species of wild flowers adorning the plains and mountains.

*The Cypriot landscape is dominated
by thick forests and rare species of flowers.*

Fauna

Cyprus has highly interesting fauna. The agrino, or mountain sheep (moufflon), is only one of the species native to the region. The male has large curved horns, and a light-brown fleece. The female does not have horns. The agrino lives for 15 to 20 years and is a very elegant, powerful beast. Their numbers have diminished considerably, especially since 1974. They now live in the forest of Paphos, a protected area in which hunting is permanently banned.

Cyprus is also home to a wide variety of birds, of which there are over 300 different kinds. Of these, 46 live permanently on the island, 27 are migratory, nesting here regularly, while 24 are occasional visitors which nest occasionally or have nested on Cyprus in the past. We may note the presence of the lammergeier, one of the rarest birds of prey in Europe, which is threatened with extinction, while other kinds that can be encountered in different parts of the island include the peregrine falcon, black francolin, and the golden eagle.

Cyprus also has some interesting wetlands, in which can be found a large variety of fish; the presence of rare serpents is a further attraction of the region. Two species of sea-turtle reproduce on the beaches of Lara: the green turtle and caretta caretta. The sea-turtles of Cyprus are protected by a Biological Station at Lara, on the basis of a programme drawn up by the Fishing Directorate; many foreign visitors come to the area each year to offer their help in preserving these rare species.

Nature lovers are highly interested in the agrino, and there are other notable kinds of fauna on the island.

HISTORY

From mythology to modern times

Mythology

The mythology of Cyprus is inextricably bound up with the goddess of love, Aphrodite. The goddess represented the embodiment of female beauty, and many Greek myths were woven around her. According to the Hesiod's Theogony, Kronos castrated his father Ouranos with a sharp sickle and cast his genitals into the ocean. A white foam formed, from which emerged a beautiful girl with gold hair – Aphrodite. And the Zephyr, with his gentle breath, carried the girl "on the waves of the sounding sea, amidst the soft foam" to Paphos on Cyprus, as we are informed by the Homeric hymn to Aphrodite. The moment the goddess set foot on land, beautiful flowers sprang up, anemones and capers, which still grow amongst the rocks at Paphos. The Hours, daughters of Zeus, at once ran to welcome Aphrodite. Cyprus thereafter became the favourite island of the goddess, where she always wanted to be:

Gorgon-head, Cypriot stater.

> "Laughter-loving Aphrodite
> went to Cyprus, to Paphos,
> where is her precinct and fragrant altar".
>
> *(Homer, Odyssey ix, 360-363)*

It was also on Cyprus that Adonis fell in love with Aphrodite. As Adonis was hunting at the western end of Cyprus, on cape Akamas, he stooped to drink water from a little lake, and espied the goddess taking her bath. This is the well-known site now called the "Baths of Aphrodite" (Loutra tis Aphroditis). Just above the sea, amidst the greenery, is the little lake in which the goddess used to bathe herself after swimming in the sea. As they gazed at each other, they fell in love. In the 12th c. BC, long before Homer composed the Iliad, the first sanctuary to Aphrodite was built at Palaipaphos. The first high-priest of the temple was Kinyras, and the high-priests after him were his descendants, the Kinyrades. Every spring a special festival called the Aphrodisia was held in honour of the goddess Aphrodite. It included sacrifices to the goddess, as well as music, poetry and athletic events. The festival, which was comparable with the Panathenaia at Athens, began with a procession led by the Kinyrades priests. This wended its way through the goddess's sacred gardens, in which all kinds of flowers were planted in thanksgiving to the goddess, and ended at the temple of Aphrodite at Palaipaphos.

*Marble statue of Aphrodite,
from Soloi. 1st century.
Archaeological Museum,
Nicosia.*

Thousands of worshippers from all over the then known world attended to honour the goddess. Another legend connected with Cyprus is the myth of Atalanta, who was abandoned by her father at birth. Atalanta grew up in the forests and became a beautiful woman, who offered to marry any man who could beat her in a foot-race. She also vowed, however, to kill the losers with her arrows. One of those who competed with her was Hippomenes, a descendant of the sea-god Poseidon. Just before the contest began, Aphrodite's son Eros shot an arrow into Atalanta's heart, whereupon she fell in love with Hippomenes, whom she begged not to take part in the contest. Unable to persuade him, or to change the terms of the race, Atalanta thought of a device to save her lover's life. She plucked three golden apples from an apple-tree on Cyprus and told Hippomenes to drop them on the ground as he ran. She then stopped to pick them up, and Hippomenes therefore won the race, to the great delight of both of them.

The legend of Pygmalion and his love for Galatea is also connected with Cyprus, and with the town of Paphos in particular. Pygmalion made an ivory statue of a woman that was so perfect that he fell in love with it.

The goddess Aphrodite took pity on him for this love and brought the statue to life, as Galatea. From the marriage of Pygmalion and Galatea was born a son, Paphos, who founded the city of this name and dedicated it to Aphrodite in gratitude for his birth. Paphos also built the first sanctuary in honour of the goddess. The present name of the island first occurs in Homer's Iliad, and there are many theories relating to its origins. One claims that it derives from the kypris, a small tree that flourishes in countries such as Egypt, Arabia and Persia, which was introduced to the island by the first settlers. Cyprus is also said to have been the name of one of the cities on the island, which was located in the north, between Kyrenia and Akanthou, according to Honorius and Isidore. The name has also been derived from the epithet kypris applied to the goddess Aphrodite. Homer calls the goddess of love Kypris. According to yet another version, Cyprus took its name from a son or daughter of the famous king Kinyras. Kinyras is mentioned in Homer, but the roots of his genealogical tree go much deeper, to the mythological past. Finally, what is perhaps the most generally accepted version argues that the word kypros means copper. This is probably an eteocypriot word, the Eteocypriots being the original, indigenous inhabitants of the island before the arrival of the Achaeans and its hellenisation. The island was named after copper because Cyprus was in fact one of the earliest places with a notable output of this metal, and its extraction and exploitation brought about a revolution in the economic life of the island.

Clay group of Eros and a goat.
Hellenistic period, Cypriot Museum, Nicosia.

Early History

The prehistory of Cyprus is divided into three major periods: the Neolithic period, the Chalcolithic period, and the Bronze Age.

Neolithic period (7000 - 3900 BC)

The earliest settlements on Cyprus date from this period, and are situated near the south and north coasts (Chirokitia, Kalavasos, Petra tou Limniti, Frenaros, etc.). Only stone objects have survived from the first phase, with pottery making its appearance after 5000 BC. The people built their houses on carefully chosen sites near rivers or hills. The houses were made of stone, clay and wood, and were circular in shape. It is clear from archaeological excavations that the people lived by hunting and fishing, while traces of primitive forms of farming and stock-breeding are also found.

Chalcolithic period (3900 - 2500 BC)

Most of the Chalcolithic settlements are on the west coast of Cyprus, where a fertility goddess was worshipped (Kisonerga, Lemba, Kalavasos, and Erimi). The inhabitants of Cyprus discovered copper during this period, but it was exploited on only a very limited scale. The earliest copper artefacts found, amongst them tools, chisels, seals, spits, fish-hooks and jewellery, date from the Chalcolithic period.

Bronze Age (2500 - 1050 BC)

During this period there was widespread use of bronze, from which Cyprus derived wealth. Commercial relations were developed with the Near East, Egypt, and the Aegean. About 1400 BC, the Mycenaeans settled on the island, initially as traders and later as colonists, bringing with them the Greek language, religion, institutions, customs and art. According to tradition, some of the heroes of the Trojan War came to the island of Cyprus when the war was over and founded city-kingdoms with imposing monuments and impressive Cyclopean walls.

Conical rhyton of faience with an enamel sheathing. Kition, 13th century BC.

Salamis was founded by Teucer, son of Telamon, Paphos by Agapenor of Arcadia, Idalion by Chalkanor, Lapethos by Praxander from Lakonia, Kyrenia by Cepheus, Kourion by the Argives, and Chytroi (Kythrea) by Chytros, while Akamas, son of Theseus gave his name to a promontory. The island was now part of the great Greek family, speaking the same language and practising the same religion, and the relationships into which it entered helped Cyprus to face the many would-be conquerors from neighbouring countries.

Historical times

The historical era on Cyprus may be divided into the **Cypro-Geometric**, **Cypro-Archaic**, **Cypro-Classical**, and the **Hellenistic** and the **Roman** periods.

Cypro-Geometric (1050 - 750 BC)

This period, during which Greek civilisation extended over the entire island, saw the emergence of the city-kingdoms, of which there were ten. The Dorian conquest of Mycenaean Greece (about 1100 BC) made it possible for the Phoenicians to gather trade into their hands and found colonies at vital points of the Mediterranean. Amongst the places they settled was Cyprus (Kition). The cultural evolution of the island was not affected however, and the 8th c. BC

Mycenaean amphoroid krater from the tomb at Enkomi. Early 4th century BC.

was a period of great prosperity. The motifs adorning the Geometric vases of the period point to the flowering of metal- and ivory-working and weaving. It was probably on Cyprus that the Greeks became acquainted with the Phoenician alphabet which, suitably adapted, gave birth to the Greek alphabet.

Cypro-Archaic period (750 - 475 BC)

Cyprus continued to prosper, but became the object of various would-be conquerors. The Cypriot kingdoms struggled to retain their independence, but fell victim one after the other to powerful foreign foes – the Assyrians, the Egyptians, and the Persians. The most important kingdom in this period was that of Salamis. The finds testify eloquently to the wealth of the Cypriot kingdoms, and also afford evidence for the survival of Mycenaean burial customs and for Cypriot social structures. During the period of Persian domination, the Cypriot kings continued to govern their kingdoms, but were obliged to pay a heavy tribute and offer naval support to the Persian forces on campaign.

Cypro-Classical period (475 - 325 BC)

A main feature of this period was the Greek struggle to liberate Cyprus from the Persians. A number of unsuccessful attempts to achieve this were made by the Athenians. The Athenian general Kimon brought a fleet of 200 ships to Cyprus in 449 BC, but was killed at the battle of Kition. In the early 4th c., Evagoras, the glorious king of Salamis, succeeded in uniting all the Cypriot kingdoms in an alliance with Athens against Persia. After a war lasting many years he was obliged to sign a peace treaty with the Persians, surrender his sovereignty over the Cypriot cities apart from Salamis, and pay tribute to the Persians. The Persian domination of the island was brought to an end by Alexander the Great (332 BC). During his great, victorious campaign, Alexander conquered Persia, and Cyprus became a part of his empire.

Hellenistic period (325 - 30 BC)

After the wars fought between Alexander's generals and successors to divide his empire, Cyprus came under the influence of the Hellenistic kingdom of the Ptolemies of Egypt, and by extension of the Greek Alexandrian world. For Cyprus, this was a period of great wealth and prosperity. The Cypriot kingdoms were dissolved and the island was unified under the Ptolemies, with the capital at Paphos. The peaceful conditions that prevailed led to an economic and cultural flowering. The important monuments dating from this period include the tombs of the kings at Paphos and the theatre at Kourion (2nd c. BC). One of the outstanding Greek intellectuals of the period was Zeno of Kition (late 3rd-early 2nd c. BC), who taught philosophy in Athens and was the founding father of the Stoic School. It was also at this time that the Greek alphabet was disseminated over the entire island.

Head of a kore statue from Idalion. Early 5th century BC.

Roman period (30 BC - AD 336)

In the wars between Egypt and Rome, Cyprus became embroiled in the final confrontation. After the defeat of Antony and Cleopatra at the battle of Actium (31 BC), Cyprus was integrated into the Roman empire and governed by a Roman proconsul, whose seat was at Paphos. During the first visit to the island of St. Paul and St. Barnabas (AD 45), the proconsul of Cyprus, Sergius Paulus, was converted to Christianity and Cyprus became the first land with a Christian governor. Many of the cities were destroyed by devastating earthquakes in the 1st c. BC and the 1st c. AD, and were subsequently rebuilt. In AD 313, the Edict of Milan secured freedom of worship for the Christian population, and in AD 325, bishops from Cyprus took part in the 1st Ecumenical Council at Nicaea. This, again, was a period of great economic and cultural prosperity. A number of important monuments are preserved from Roman times, including theatres (Salamis, Soloi and Kourion, which was rebuilt and enlarged), temples (of

Mosaic from the house of Eustolios at Kourion.

Apollo Hylates at Kourion, and of Zeus at Salamis), sanctuaries dedicated to Asklepios, the father of medicine, which also functioned as sanatoria, and also private dwellings with mosaics (house of Eustolios at Kourion, and houses of Dionysos, Orpheus, Theseus, and Aion at Paphos).

Marble statue of a sleeping Eros. 1st century BC. Archaeological Museum, Nicosia.

Medieval times

Byzantine period (AD 330 - 1191)

When the Roman empire was divided into the Eastern and Western empires, Cyprus became part of the former, which is known as the Byzantine empire. More earthquakes in the 4th c. AD completely destroyed the major cities, which were abandoned, and replaced by new foundations. The capital was moved to Constantia, near Salamis. During the 4th and 5th centuries, large basilicas were erected.

In AD 488, the tomb of St. Barnabas was discovered at Salamis, along with his relic and the manuscript Gospel of St. Matthew, and the emperor Zeno granted the church of Cyprus complete autonomy. The archbishop received imperial privileges, and was allowed, for example, to carry an imperial sceptre instead of a pastoral staff, to wear a red imperial cloak, and to sign in red ink. This period was dominated architecturally by Early Christian basilicas, which had three or five aisles. Remains of these structures have been discovered all over Cyprus, the most important being the three-aisled basilicas of Ayia Triada at Yalousa, Ayios Varnavas, the Panayia Kanakaria, Ayios Iraklidios at Tamasos, and Ayios Yeoryios at Peyia, and the five-aisled basilicas of Ayios Epiphanios at Constantia and Ayia Kyriaki at Kato Paphos.

Several mosaics are also preserved from this period, which are of unique quality and style and are of great value because of their rarity. Very few examples of mosaics are preserved from this period from anywhere within the Byzantine empire, because all anthropomorphic depictions were destroyed during the iconoclastic controversy. In AD 647, the Arabs, under their leader Mu'awiyah, made their first destructive raid on Cyprus. For three centuries after this, the Arabs and the pirates plagued the island until the emperor Nikephoros Phokas vanquished them and liberated Cyprus in AD 965. With this final defeat of the Arabs, Cyprus became a province of

Mosaic floor in the ruins of the church of Ayios Yeoryios at Peyia.

the Byzantine empire once more, with its capital now at Nicosia. The Komnini showed great interest in the defence of the island. After the conquest of Asia Minor by the Turks, Cyprus became an advanced outpost of Byzantium. At this time, the castles of St. Hilarion, Buffavento, and Kantara were built in the Pentadaktylos range, to control the northern part of the island. Many monasteries were also founded at this period, including the Panayia Kykkou, Ayios Ioannis Chrysostomos, Macheras monastery, Ayios Neophytos, Ayios Nikolaos tis Stegis, the Panayia tou Araka, Asinou monastery, and others. The building of so many monasteries is an indication that monasticism was flourishing on the island, and that the people had a strongly religious bent. Veneration of the Virgin (Panayia) was particularly pronounced, and many monasteries were dedicated to her.

Richard the Lionheart and the Knights Templar (AD 1191 - 1192)

Richard the Lionheart, king of England, took part in the Third Crusade. In 1191 one of his ships, on board which was his fiancée Berengaria of Navarre, his sister, and other important persons, was wrecked near Limassol. Isaac Komninos, the Byzantine governor who had proclaimed himself emperor of the island, refused assistance to the shipwrecked party.

This offensive behaviour by Isaac enraged Richard, and gave him an "excuse" to capture the island in 1191. He married Berengaria in Limassol and crowned her queen of England. Shortly afterwards, he sold Cyprus to the Knights Templar for 100,000 dinars, but after the inhabitants of the island rose against them, they sold it in their turn the following year to Francis Guy de Lusignan, exiled king of Jerusalem. This event ushered in a new period in Cypriot history, the period of Frankish rule.

Frankish period (12th - 15th c.)

Guy de Lusignan introduced the feudal system into Cyprus, dividing the island up into fiefs and distributing them to European nobles. The local inhabitants became villeins. The Catholic church became the official church and attempted, with the collusion of the political authorities, to suppress the Greek Orthodox church of Cyprus. Despite the intense pressure, the laity and the churchmen continued to adhere to Orthodoxy. Privileges were granted to foreign merchants (from Venice, Genoa, Marseilles, and elsewhere), making Famagusta one of the most important ports in the eastern Mediterranean. Nicosia was the capital of the island and the seat of the Frankish king.

The Frankish period came to an end when the last queen, Caterina Cornaro ceded the kingdom to Venice in 1489, in return for a life pension. There are some important examples of Gothic ecclesiastical architecture on the island, including the cathedral of Ayia Sophia in Nicosia, the church of Ayios Nikolaos at Famagusta, and the abbey of Bellapais in the area of Kyrenia. The Franks also renovated, enlarged and strengthened many of the defensive works, such as the castles of St. Hilarion, Buffavento, and Kantara. Fortification walls were built in the cities and strengthened with towers (Nicosia, Famagusta, and Kyrenia). and the castle of Kolossi was erected near Limassol.

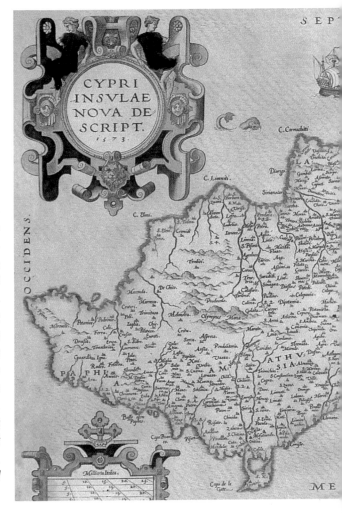

Early Modern history
Venetian period (1489 - 1571)

Cyprus became a Venetian province for about a century, during which the growing Ottoman threat obliged the Venetians further to improve the defences of the island.In Nicosia they demolished the fortifications erected by the Lusignans and reduced the size of the town, to make its defences more effective. Entrance to the town was by way of three gates: the Kyrenia gate, the Paphos gate, and the Famagusta gate.

Turkish period (1571 - 1878)

The new Venetian fortification works failed to protect Cyprus against the Ottoman Turks. In 1570, Turkish forces launched an attack on Cyprus, captured Nicosia, and slaughtered 20,000 of the inhabitants. They then proceeded to lay siege to Famagusta for a year. In 1571, after noble resistance by its defenders, Famagusta surrendered to the Turkish pasha Lala Mustafa; despite his promise to permit the defenders to depart freely, he had the garrison commander, Marcantonio Bragadino savagely tortured and put to death, and all the rest were executed. After the Turkish conquest, the Catholic clergy were either expelled, or converted to Islam, but the Orthodox church was rehabilitated and the archbishop was recognised by the Sublime Porte as representative of the Greek orthodox population. The office of dragoman was introduced and formed a link between the Greek inhabitants and the Turkish administration. Amongst the important duties of the dragoman were the registering of Greek property, and the allocation and collection of taxes.

The most important of the dragomans of Cyprus was Chatziyorgakis Kornesios, who enjoyed great wealth and political power, and greatly assisted the subjugated Greeks in a variety of ways. In the end, he was beheaded in Constantinople, a victim of the machinations of his opponents. Cyprus experienced very difficult times during the years of Turkish domination. When the Greek national uprising against the Turks began in 1821, archbishop Kyprianos was executed, along with other members of the clergy and hundreds of ordinary citizens (9 July 1821). During this period many Christian churches were converted into mosques, including those of Ayia Sophia in Nicosia, and Ayios Nikolaos at Famagusta. Public baths (hammams) and inns (hania) were built; it is of note that during the three hundred years of Turkish rule, only one paved road was laid, linking Larnaca with Nicosia.

Old map of Cyprus Antwerp 1575.

Period of British rule (1878 - 1960)

In 1878, after a special agreement with the Ottoman empire, Great Britain took over the administration of Cyprus, which formally remained part of the Ottoman empire until 1914. At this date Great Britain annexed the island, because the Ottoman empire entered the First World War on the side of Germany. The Cypriots welcomed the transfer of authority to Britain with great joy, in the belief that at some point in the future the British would cede the island to Greece, as had happened with the Ionian islands in 1864. In 1923, Turkey signed the Treaty of Lausanne and gave up all claims to Cyprus, which was proclaimed a British colony in 1925. After the arrival of the British on Cyprus, the administrative system was radically reformed and the basis was laid for a well-organised civil service. The lawcourts were modernised with the introduction of an impartial legal system, and judicial institutions were consolidated. This put an end to the abuse of state institutions that had been a feature of the Turkish period. During the Second World War, thousands of Cypriots fought as volunteers in Greece and on the British side on many fronts. After the War, however, the British refused the Cypriots the right of self-government which it had ceded to other peoples. After all peaceful, political means had been exhausted, an armed liberation struggle by EOKA (National Organisation of Cypriot Freedom-fighters) began in 1955. The British reacted by passing special emergency powers acts. They built detention centres in which they held anyone suspected of being involved in the liberation struggle, and filled the jails with political prisoners. The insurgents faced terrible torture and were sent to the gallows, offering their lives as the price of their love for their native land. During this liberation struggle (1957-58) the first clashes took place between Greek Cypriots and Turkish Cypriots. As soon as the armed struggle began in 1955, Britain invited Greece and Turkey to a tripartite conference to discuss the question. This conference ended in failure, but, significantly, Turkey had been invited to discuss the Cypriot question as an equal party to the discussion. The meeting was followed by Greek-Turkish negotiations that ended in the Zurich and London agreements of 1959 and the creation of the Republic of Cyprus in 1960.

Greek priests bless the British flag in Nicosia. Gennadeios Library, Athens.

Republic of Cyprus (1960 - present)

On the basis of the Zurich and London agreements, Cyprus was proclaimed an independent republic on 16 August 1960. Cyprus is a member of the UN, the Council of Europe, the Commonwealth, and the Organisation of Non-aligned States. Also on the basis of these agreements, Great Britain maintains two sovereign military bases on Cyprus, one of 158.4 square km. at Dekelia and the other in the area of Akrotiri-Episkopi.

The Constitution of the Republic of Cyprus proved unworkable, however, and could not be fully implemented. In 1963, therefore, the President of the Republic proposed a number of amendments. The Turkish community rose in revolt, the Turkish Cypriot ministers withdrew from the Council of Ministers, Turkish Cypriot civil servants did not go to work, and Turkey threatened to invade the island.

Since the beginning of 1964 there has been a United Nations peace-keeping force on the island, following a decision passed by the Security Council. Ever since, Turkey has not ceased to scheme against the independence and territorial integrity of the Cypriot Republic. The Turkish Cypriot leadership, acting on the instructions of the Turkish government, has worked since this time to secure the partition of Cyprus and its annexation to Turkey.

In July 1974, the military dictatorship of Greece organised a coup in Cyprus against President Makarios. On 20 July of this year, Turkey invaded Cyprus with an army of 40,000.

The National Guard, weakened by the coup, was unable to mount an effective defence. The Turkish forces initially occupied a small area in the province of Kyrenia, which they extended during the course of the ceasefire. The talks begun at Geneva ended in an impasse and the Turks took further military action on 14 August, occupying 37.6 % of the territory of Cyprus. Two hundred thousand Greek-Cypriots were displaced from their homes and sought refuge in the unoccupied

Emblem of the Republic of Cyprus.

areas, becoming refugees in their own country and turning to all sorts of crime. Another tragic consequence of the invasion was the destruction of the cultural heritage and the alteration of the demographic composition of the island. Churches, monasteries, and archaeological treasures were looted and pillaged, and only a small number of Greek Cypriots were allowed to remain in Karpasia.

Despite the international outcry and condemnation of Turkey for the invasion of the island, Turkish armies still occupy the north part of Cyprus, and in 1983, an illegal Turkish Cypriot state was founded in the occupied areas, which has been recognised only by Turkey.

The Green Line resulted in the destruction of a centuries-old tradition. Thousands of Turkish settlers were planted in the occupied territories and usurped the property of the Greek Cypriots; the Attila Line divides the island in two and runs through the heart of Nicosia, which is thus the only European capital to remain divided.

4

CULTURE & TRADITION

Literature - Arts - Culural Events - Customs & Way of life
Marriage - Song & Dance - Costumes - People & Professions

*The art and wisdom of the ordinary people
of Cyprus are cultural factors,
and are carefully guarded.*

The entire atmosphere of Cyprus is redolent of refined aesthetic taste and well-developed artistic sensitivity. From the very first pages of its history, Cyprus can boast of some significant manifestations of culture and civilisation, starting with the earliest organised communities of the Neolithic period and continuing into the later historical periods. The flowering of trade (mainly in copper), shipbuilding and seafaring, and relations with neighbouring peoples created the conditions for the evolution of an authentic "Cypriot" art. The development of this art over the centuries reveals two main features: the large number of foreign influences that were successfully assimilated to create an original, typically Cypriot art, and a conservatism in changing adopting new forms. Cyprus is one of the few parts of the Mediterranean where specific styles and forms were retained and preferred for long periods of time.

Over the course of the troubled history of the island, the many conquerors failed to prevent the cultural and artistic flowering of Cyprus. Poets and chroniclers created a notable body of literature — so much so that the first renaissance of Greek literature may be said to have taken place on Cyprus. Cypriot folk poets hymned the ideals of the fatherland and of bravery in the person of Diyenis Akritas, a symbol of safety and protection against the Saracens with whom Cypriots sought to identify as a brave, noble warrior.

The Cypriot tradition also includes a rich folk art. Ancient techniques were handed on from generation to generation, and are still practised today by skilled craftsmen. The industrious Cypriots converted the material proffered in such abundance by the land into outstanding works of folk art, such as pottery, wood-carving, metalwork, basket-weaving, weaving (Phythkiotika), embroidery (Lefkaritika), religious painting and so on. Cypriots proudly preserve their way of life and customs, many of which are rooted in antiquity. this can be seen clearly at the various festivals and celebrations on the island. The polite, hospitable inhabitants of the island, with their sociable, outgoing manners, always take visitors along with them to their celebrations.

Cypriots are a very religious people, as is attested by the many churches and monasteries, especially those devoted to the Virgin, and by the large number of religious festivals.

The archaeological sites and finds from ancient Cyprus clearly indicate the belief of the inhabitants in the ancient deities, while Byzantine Cyprus, and Early Christian Cyprus before it, are eloquent in their testimony to the smooth continuity with which the ancient gods were succeeded by Christ and Aphrodite by the Virgin. Examples of art from these periods have survived to the present day in a very good state of preservation. The monasteries of Macheras, Stavrovouni, and Ayios Neophytos are only a few of the many scattered throughout the island. They are normally located at sites offering visitors a panoramic view, and partly hidden amongst the lavish greenery. There are also many notable churches, famous for their outstanding wall-paintings, many of which have well survived their travels through time and have been preserved to us in very good condition. In the villages in the mountains of Cyprus one frequently encounters stone settlements that exude peace and tranquillity, and are therefore popular for summer holidays. Generally speaking Cypriot architecture reflects the vicissitudes experienced by the island over the centuries, as well as the high aesthetic sense of the islanders, who succeeded in overcoming all difficulties. As one wanders in the towns and villages of the island, one has a feeling of being suspended in time; the signs of modern life are to be found amongst the incense-burners of past centuries.

UNESCO has included nine of the churches in the Troodos range, and some of the villages, in its catalogue of the World Cultural Heritage, both on account of the superb art of their icons and wall-paintings, and for their architecture.

In Cyprus everything, from its myths and history to the way in which people chose to build their houses and churches, helps to create an atmosphere of tranquillity and devotion.

Literature

Cypriot **literature** is an organic part of Greek letters. In ancient times and during the Middle Ages, the products of Cypriot writing played a leading role in Greek literature. During ancient times, the local cult of Aphrodite and its festivals furnished subjects and motifs that influenced Greek literature and art. At the same time, epic poetry evolved in Cyprus and Stasinos's Cypriot Epics exercised a major influence on both contemporary and later writers. During the Middle Ages, Cypriot love **songs** opened up new horizons for Greek literature. Poets and chroniclers created a notable body of literature and the first renaissance of Greek literature took place on Cyprus, much earlier than the Cretan renaissance in the 17th c. Poetry was the most flourishing form of literature on the island.

The themes were beauty and the nobler aspects of life, sometimes rendered with the naivety and spontaneity of the simple folk singer, and sometimes with the elevated, philosophical truth of the artistic, cultured **poet**. Medieval Cypriot folk poetry is represented mainly by the akritika songs, dealing with the feats of Diyenis Akritas on the frontiers of the Byzantine empire. Cypriot folk poets hymned the ideal of the fatherland and bravery at a time when many akrites ("frontiersmen") crossed from Asia Minor to Cyprus, bringing with them a spirit of resistance, heroism and self-sacrifice. The Cypriot songs are thought to be amongst the finest in the Greek cycle of akritika.

Diyenis Akritas was the ideal model, a symbol of security for the Cypriots in the face of the Saracen raids. The famous medieval ballad of Arodaphnousa is a love song, dealing with the love of the Lusignan king Peter I for the Cypriot girl Arodaphnousa. From the 14th c. onwards, the Frankish administration of Cyprus began to he Hellenised to some degree, for the Greek population had such great vitality that it gradually conquered the Frankish conquerors. Greek men of letters, such as Leontios Macheras and Yeoryios Boustronios, exercised great influence over the royal court on the island.

Leontios Macheras was an outstanding chronicler, and his work "Account of the sweet land of Cyprus" is a classical text of Greek literature in general. The laws of the Frankish kings of Jerusalem were translated into Greek, and a learned literature began to evolve on the island alongside the popular works.

The cultural renaissance of the Frankish period (12th-15th c.) was supplemented by a notable **religious literature**. St. Neophytos Enkleistos (12th c.) wrote church hymns, and Gregory II of Cyprus, Patriarch of Constantinople (13th c.) wrote encomia. Ilarion Kigalas, one of the most prolific of the ecclesiastical writers and archbishop of Cyprus about 1660 wrote the poem The "Lament of Cyprus", a work in the Cypriot dialect containing a large number of "purifying" elements. The 19th c. literature of Cyprus is of great interest, with the emergence of poets such as **Vasilis Michailidis**, who wrote unashamedly patriotic poems in the Cypriot dialect. Others who wrote in the Cypriot dialect include Dimitris Lipertis, Pavlos Liasidis, and Andonis Klokkaris.

Of the vast number of names representative of modern Cypriot literature, the most important are: N. Nikolaidis, Ant. Indianos, N. Kranidiotis, G. Lefkis, M. Roussia, X. Lysiotis, G. Philippou, L. Akritas, L. Pavlidis, Andis Pernaris, M. Frangoudis, and Emilios Chourmouzios. Most of them present their work in the pages of the literary journals Avgi, Kypriaka Grammata, and Paphos, or the bulletins of the Society for Cypriot Studies and the Greek Cultural Association of Cyprus. Other young writers later emerged through the pages of the journals Pnevmatiki Kypros and Kypriaka Chronika.

The Cypriot struggle for liberation and the recent events of the Turkish invasion of 1974 have given a fresh impulse to literature and created the conditions for a great literary flowering.

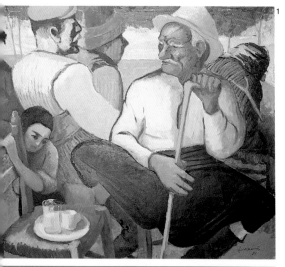

The Arts

The **visual arts** also have their place on Cyprus. From the beginning of the 20th c. Cypriot artists have painted scenes from the rural life of the island, as well as landscapes in which they have caught the continually shifting light and moods of the island with great sensitivity. An important collection of paintings from the early decades of the 20th c. to the present day is contained in the National Collection of Modern Art, which is housed in a neoclassical building in Nicosia.

Contemporary currents in painting and sculpture are also to be found in the work of many local artists, who exhibit their works in large or small art galleries, of which there are several in Nicosia, and some in the other towns on Cyprus. The list of important Cypriot painters includes Diamantis, Chr. Savvas, Koullis, Mich. Kasialos, Kanthou, G. Skoteinos, P. Georgiou, Chambis, I. Kissonergis, V. Kapos, Frangoulidis, Photiadis, Th. Rossidou-Jones and many others.

The Cypriot people has had an instinctive feel for art ever since it first conquered the island. This is an age-old legacy of its Greek descent, whose tradition has been handed down from generation to generation without interruption to the present day.

Shepherds and farmers carve the staff, the sickle, and the flute with artistic designs resembling those of the Geometric period that can be still seen on ancient Cypriot vases. With his fine knife he carves the kolotzia — round long-necked gourds — with beautiful decorative patterns and multifigural compositions drawn from rural life. The peasant puts all his soul into his vourka — the large sheepskin bag in which he keeps his provisions when he goes to the farm — adorning it with coloured beads and tassels.

1. Painting by Diamantis
   from the National Collection of Modern Art.
2. Shepherd wearing traditional costume.

The **potter's art** is widely practised in Cyprus and ranges from the simplest kouzes (cylindrical pitchers) to the most original decorative plates, flower vases, dinner sets, and so on. The art of **wood-carving**, which dates from the Byzantine period, is also highly developed on Cyprus. The precious, elaborately carved iconostases of the churches and monasteries, the old furniture, wooden cupboards, chests with double-headed eagles and rosettes, the tsaeres — heavy bridal chairs — flower-bedecked shelves and other wood-carved objects are the work of Cypriot taliadoroi, who were formerly unrivalled in their work both in Nicosia and other areas that are now Turkish-occupied. The same may be said of the working of bronze, gold and silver.

1, 3. The church of Ayios Ioannis Theologos near the Archbishop's Residence: the iconostasis and archbishop's throne, with a detail of the double-headed eagle.
2. Goldsmith at work.

Women's handicrafts are a prominent product of folk art. The women of the island have worked in silk-production and weaving from very early times, working with the cocoon and using the old looms to produce the famous silks, linen itaredes, woollen rugs, and coloured, striped upholstery fabrics, curtains and table cloths, the greatest exponents of the art being the women of Lefkoniko (now in occupied Cyprus).

The finest example of women's handicraft, however, are the famous laces and embroideries known as Lefkaritika, made by the women of Lefkara, a village in the province of Larnaca.

Lefkaritika lace was formerly made of local linen, but is now made of a finer, imported version. It is used to adorn sheets, cushion-covers and pillow-cases, table-cloths, towels, tray-covers, curtains, and so on. The technique is based on the weaving of the fabric, and the patterns are accordingly strictly geometrical in character, formed by bold horizontal and vertical lines.

Lefkaritika lace evolved from an earlier form of Cypriot embroidery known as asproploumia, which were very similar to the old embroideries of the countries in the eastern Mediterranean.

Working at the loom.

An important role was played in this development by the Venetian presence on Cyprus. The lace is an expression of the place, that has survived through time, and the kinds, techniques, materials, motifs, and names reveal signs left by the past, that stamp the Cypriot identity.

The Phythkiotika textiles are another superb example of Cypriot handicraft. This is the best-known kind of Cypriot textile, and takes its name from the village of Phyti, in the province of Paphos, where they were mainly made.

The characteristic features of these textiles are their coloured, geometric, relief patterns, or ploumia, worked on cotton fabric in a natural colour. The ploumia have bright, basic colours — blue, red, green, orange, and yellow— and are worked during the weaving of the fabric, by using coloured threads, or phitilia, which are set amongst the threads of the warp. The predominant shape used for the ploumia is the lozenge, in different versions, rows of which are set parallel with the narrow sides of the fabric. Descriptive names drawn from everyday life are given to the ploumia, such as "black-eye", "teacher's shoe", and so on. The most common use of the Phythkiotika patterns was on rectangular kerchiefs, though they were also found on larger items, such as bed covers and table-cloths.

We should also note here the tsetsoi, large, shallow baskets, with an inconceivable variety of cheerful, coloured stylised patterns, which were used by villagers as fruit-bowls, or to decorate the walls of their houses.

Examples of the Phythkiotika textiles and Lefkaritika embroideries that adorn Cypriot houses.

Cultural events

Various cultural events take place on Cyprus all the year round, involving local and foreign artists. There are also many church festivals and feast-days, and Cypriots generally lose no opportunity to display their sociability and their love of life and entertainment.

One of the major celebrations is the wine festival, which takes place every September in the town of Limassol, in the Municipal Gardens. It includes a number of different events, such as concerts, lectures, Cypriot and other Greek traditional dances, and a trade fair. Wine is served free of charge, and thousands of locals and foreigners visit the festival to enjoy themselves and get to know the Bacchus of Limassol.

Carnival is celebrated in Limassol, and recently also in Paphos. There are parades of kantadoroi, dancing by people wearing costumes, and competitions for the best costume. The celebrations culminate in the parade of floats on the last Sunday of Carnival.

In May, every town celebrates its own flower festival, or anthesteria, with parades and competitions for the best flower composition.

Before the Turkish invasion in 1974, the Orange festivals of Famagusta and Morphou were also famous.

Πιννε κρασιν νασινς ζωνν

1, 2. Scenes from the wine festival at Limassol.
3. Orange festival at Famagusta,
   before the Turkish invasion.
4, 5. Scenes from the flower festival.

3

4

5

Customs and way of life

Cypriots are very attached to the past and continue to practise their ancestral customs.

The **festival of Lights** is celebrated with great brilliance in Cyprus, as in Greece. When the church service is over, everyone takes holy water in containers that they have brought with them specially for this purpose. They also take the holy light, and in this way, the divine light illuminates every house. Every room has to have a lighted candle, whose peaceful flame will overcome all "temptations". The holy water is used afterwards to spray all the gardens and vines, where there are any. When they get home, the housewife makes the traditional loukoumades. The custom is to throw the first of these straight from the frying pan on to the roof of the house, to drive away evil spirits.

"Before you go, eat a piece of brown-fry,
Sausage, (cut with) a black-handled knife."

In Cyprus, as in other parts of Greece, Easter and the resurrection of Christ are celebrated with great religious piety and brilliance. On Good Friday, the Epitaphios is carried in procession. Before the Epitaphios is brought out of the church, the faithful pay reverence to it and pass beneath it one by one, and the priest distributes the flowers from it. The iconostasis and all the icons in the church are covered with black or mauve cloth. On Easter Saturday morning, the cloths are removed so that the icons can be seen again, and the church is decorated with festive ribbons. On Easter Saturday, housewives make flaounes, a traditional Easter food to be found in every Cypriot house. It is a kind of bread roll stuffed with a mixture of eggs, cheese and currants. On Easter Saturday evening, fires are lit in the church yards and an effigy of Judas is burned. At midnight, everyone holds a taper and hears the "good word" — that is, "Christ is risen", after which they light their taper from the holy light of the priest's candlestick. Back at home, the housewives serve the traditional egg-lemon chicken soup. The celebration and feasting continues on Sunday afternoon with the traditional roasting of a lamb on a spit.

Easter at Ayia Napa.

The **festival of the Flood** is identical with Pentecost, which has its origins in the Aphrodisia — ancient rituals in honour of Aphrodite emerging from the sea. During the two days of Pentecost, trade fairs and other events, including poetry competitions, nautical competitions, exhibitions, and so on, are held in the streets on the coast.

In former times, the festival of the Flood was celebrated with particular brilliance in the town of Larnaca. Traders and pedlars from all over Cyprus, and even from Syria, brought their wares and filled the quay with their temporary shops. There were also a variety of games and other entertainments to amuse children and grown-ups alike.

In the mountain villages and the wine-producing villages, it is the custom after the end of the vintage, to make the well-known **palouze** (must-jelly). It is baked in a large pot called the chartzin. **Soutziouko** is made by first taking almond or chestnut crumbs and putting them in water; when they have become soft, they are spread in a row on a fine, but strong string. This is then tied to a hanger, consisting of a forked branch with a small hooked shoot at the top by which it is hung up. The strings are then dipped into the baked must-jelly and hung up to dry. The soutziouko has to be dipped 6-8 times before taking its final form. The making of the palouze serves as an opportunity for social contact.

The **custom of smoking** is a survival from ancient times. It is practised only by women, and in all kinds of situations. The evil eye, or vaskania, can be averted by smoking, which involves the burning of olive leaves on charcoals. Every house has its hand-smoker, which may be of silver, bronze or clay. The woman or daughter of the house "smokes" it every Sunday evening. Those who happen to be in the house at the time waft the smoke nearer with their hand and make the sign of the cross. Before people set out on a journey, or when they return, they "smoke" their fellow travellers, and strangers are also "smoked" when they arrive and when they depart.

Marriage

Marriage has its own history in Cyprus. The most common way to get married was formerly through match-making. The proposal was made by the groom's family, and it was considered demeaning if it was made by the family of the bride. The match-making "season" was during Carnival and in the week before Lent. There was, of course, some disappointment if these days passed without anything happening.

The Carnival is come
Lent is at hand
And the girls are without a man.

Weddings were invariably held on Sunday. The ceremonial started the previous Thursday, however, with the stuffing of the bed. All the bride's friends helped to stuff the bridal mattress. The hair used to stuff it was first taken to the spring to be washed. When it had dried, it was brought to the house where everyone began to sew, singing and laughing.

When the sewing was completed, four crosses were placed at the corners of the bed, to the accompaniment of a song. *"Place four crosses and four bells, so that the bride and groom will sleep the sleep of the blessed".* When all was finished, the mattress was taken to the house of the bride-to-be, and her entire dowry was put in baskets and placed where everyone could see it. On the Saturday, seven of the bride's friends filled their baskets with corn and, having washed it, took it to the bride's house to prepare the wedding food, or resi — boiled corn and lamb. On the Sunday, the dressing of the bride began at 12 o'clock. Her clothes were brought to her in baskets by her friends, while outside, the dance of the clothes was played by violinists. When the dance was over, the dressing of the bride began.

"A good day, a beautiful day, a blessed day
May the work we have begun be solidly done.
Today shines the heaven, today shines the day
Today they're getting married, and so is the dove. "

When the bride was dressed, the bride's mother was summoned. The moment when the daughter left her home was a very emotional one. The bride was then escorted to the church by her father, accompanied by music. When the sacrament was over, the couple were escorted home. The groom's mother was waiting in the house to cense the newly-weds and give the groom a pomegranate to break, symbolising prosperity, success and strength. This was followed by dancing, and when the bride and groom danced they were "adorned" by everyone. The newly-weds danced the "dance of the married couple", while everyone pinned banknotes to their garments. In the evening of the wedding day, there were usually singing competitions, in which the person who improvised the best couplet about the wedding or the bride and groom received enthusiastic applause. The men usually danced separately from the women. One very common dance was the antikristos (face-to-face), which was danced in couples, one couple at a time. The typical woman's dance consisted most often of movements of the open hands, accompanied by slow, almost imperceptible, repeated movements of the body, with the feet scarcely leaving the ground. The faces of the dancers had to be serious, and the head was stooped slightly towards the ground. The men danced the antikristos more wildly. The individual male dance was performed as vigorously as possible. Three or four men, holding each other by the shoulder, danced a syrtos, pulling the dancer on to the floor, before withdrawing and leaving him to perform his movements. Very skilled dancers would twist like acrobats and throw knives in the air, catching them as they fell. Afterwards, men and women danced a lively syrtos together. Not all the old customs are still observed.

1. The happy bride and groom being sprinkled with rose-water.
2. The groom being shaved, to the acoompaniment of violins.
3. Preparing the bed.
4. The newly-weds dancing, covered in banknotes.

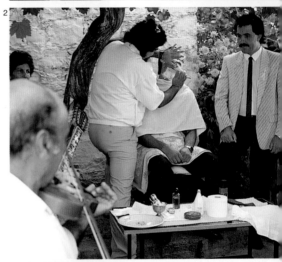

Song and Dance

Song and dance are directly linked with the lives of Cypriots. Cypriot folk-songs may be divided into akritika songs, distichs and epic songs.

The akritika cycle revolves around the legend of Diyenis Akritas, and refers to his life, feats, and death, and countless heroic incidents. The songs of the Cypriot cycle constitute a living cultural monument; despite the existence of different versions, the central idea is the same, and exudes the spirit of heroism and self-sacrifice characteristic of the Greek soul. The Cypriot distichs are a pure form of folk-poetry, reflecting every expression of the popular psyche. Like the Cretan mandinades and the distichs of the Dodecanese, they have a rare expressive range, with the Cypriot fifteen-syllable verses containing some completely original words. At weddings, festivals, feast-days, at times of joy and times of grief, the folk poets of Cyprus enliven the atmosphere with their quick-witted couplets. The music was extemporised at the same time as the verses. The violin and laouto — a kind of lute — are the indispensable instruments, played to the rhythm of a kind of tambourine made of leather on one side, which was struck with two small sticks. The final form of poetry consists of the Cypriot Epics, the most important and best known being the Arodaphnousa, a variant of the Greek word rododaphni (oleander). Dance, like song, is another form of expression for the Cypriot people. The different roles of the two sexes are mirrored in Cypriot folk dance in a manner rarely matched. In the strictly male dances, Cypriots dance spiritedly and vigorously, as though they are trying to fly. Their boots stamp thunderously on the ground, their breeches shake, and their chests are constrained proudly in their waistcoats. Female dances are an opportunity for the display of feminine modesty and submission. The girls move forwards in pairs, taking short steps, sometimes hand in hand and sometimes holding kerchiefs. During the dance, their gentle movements and gestures form a "narrative" of the events of the women's world: embroidery, housework, concern for and obedience to her husband. One distinctive dance is the sickle dance, and there is also an incredible dance performed with twelve glasses on the head.

Cypriot dance group.

Costumes

Both the male and female costumes of Cyprus are of a purely Greek character, in terms of both their form and their decoration. The **male costume** is called vrakopoukamiso. The formal dress consists of a shirt, the sovrako, and breeches, with the sovrako being replaced by the zimbouni or patsali for every-day wear. The costume is completed by a waistcoat, woollen sash, large boots, called podines, and a red fez, around the bottom of which a kerchief is wound. Finally, a large shawl is tied around the neck. There are two types of **female costume**: the bressiasti, a costume with a highly pleated skirt, and the sayia, a full-length dress, open at the front. The sayia consists of a chemise with long, flaring sleeves, and has distinctive decoration of coloured beads called petroudes. A red silk kerchief, the zonin, was tied around the waist on top of the sayia, and two more kerchiefs were tied around the head. White socks called tsourapia were worn on the feet, with light shoes, or yemenia, in the house, and kottoures for the street. The formal dress was completed by a sash, a coloured silk kerchief, and jewellery.

A traditional Cypriot costume.

People and professions

In recent decades, Cyprus has experienced unprecedented growth. Many, indeed, speak of an "economic miracle". Statistics reveal that the average per capita income, and other economic and social indexes, are comparable with those of the most advanced countries of the Western World. From having a purely agricultural economy in the 1950s and 1960s, Cyprus has progressed rapidly to being a successful industrialised country. Despite the severe shock it suffered in 1974 with the Turkish invasion and the loss of the richest territories of the Republic of Cyprus, the economy of free Cyprus recovered its prosperity, thanks to a variety of factors. The most flourishing sector was and is **tourism**.

Cyprus, the land of hospitality, where the past is respected.

Investment in infrastructure works, and the high-quality services provided by Cyprus have together made the island highly attractive to foreign companies. Since the middle of the 1980s, many foreign companies have established themselves in Cyprus, including banks, insurance companies, real estate and architecture companies, consultants, and so on.

At the same time the inhabitants of the villages continue to work in **farming** and **stock-raising**. The produce of the island includes its famous citrus fruits, potatoes, especially a kind of sweet potato called kolokasi, bananas and grapes.

Agricultural work is often hard and tiring, but produces select produce like the kolokasi (fig. 2, 3) and oranges (fig. 4) of Cyprus.

Viticulture was widely practised in ancient times and still provides work for one quarter of the rural population. The Lusignans placed great importance on the growing of vines and the making of wine that they advertised as the best in the world. The most common varieties of grape are the black and the white, or xynisteri, as it is known locally. Other traditional varieties are the Mouskato, the Oftarmo and the Spourtiko, which produce excellent wine.

The oldest, most characteristic Cypriot wine is Koumandaria. Brandy and various liqueurs, such as zivania, the Cypriot version of tsipouro, are also common.

The cultivation of vines and wine-making are very popular occupations amongst the inhabitants of Cyprus.

Fishing, too, is widely practised on Cyprus; in addition to the seas, which are rich in fish stocks, there are private fish-farms that satisfy the greater part of local demand.

Within the sphere of **stock-breeding**, the raising of cows, birds, sheep and goats, and pigs is common, and in recent years the rearing of rabbits has been introduced. The output of beef, veal, lamb and goat-meat does not fully satisfy local demand, which is met by imports from abroad.

Fishing and stock-raising are fairly common ways of earning a living.

Cypriots also work as **potters** and **wood-carvers**, traditional professions that are still flourishing at the present day. Vases and dinner-sets are decorated with original designs, and wood-carved artefacts adorn the iconostases of the churches and domestic furniture. Cyprus is also renowned for its **weaving** and **women's handicrafts**. Embroideries and lace, bedspreads and sheets, are all made with characteristic Cypriot skill. The lefkaritika embroideries from Lefkara are famous, as are the phythkiotika textiles with coloured decorative designs.

Cypriots are hospitable, generous people who will invite you into their house with the familiar kopiaste (come in); once you have entered they will do their best to please you, insisting — occasionally to excess — that you take whatever they are offering. Parents strive until a ripe old age to help their children, their first concern being to give them the best possible education. The proportion of people with a university education is one of the highest in the world. This circumstance, and the lack until recently of a university on the island, made the Cypriots a very cosmopolitan people, who travelled abroad to attend foreign universities.

Most of them go to Greece, Britain, and America. The University of Cyprus was founded a few years ago.

It is a pleasant surprise to foreigners to find that there is no communication problem, since most Cypriots speak English to a satisfactory level, either because they belong to the modern generation who have been taught English, or because they migrated and lived for many years in Britain.

Until the 1950s many Cypriots migrated for economic reasons to Britain, Australia, America and elsewhere. In these countries there are large Cypriot communities who retain strong links with the home country. In the villages, and to some extent also in the towns, Cypriot society is still a traditional, male-dominated society.

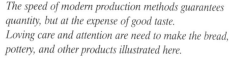

The speed of modern production methods guarantees quantity, but at the expense of good taste.
Loving care and attention are need to make the bread, pottery, and other products illustrated here.

5

MONUMENTS & SIGHTS

Museums - Churches - Monasteries - Archaeological sites
Castles - Mosaics - Beauty spots

One of the impressive aspects of a visit to Cyprus is the fact that so many cultural monuments, memories of the ages-old history of the island, are crowded into so small an area. This unique cultural tapestry comprises prehistoric settlements, ancient Greek temples, Byzantine churches and monasteries with their outstanding mosaics and wall-paintings, Crusader castles, Gothic churches, and Venetian forts. The following guide is appended to make it easier for visitors to enjoy it, and also the enchanting, tranquil natural environment, as they walk the pathways amidst unique beauty and tranquillity. It consists of a list of the monuments and sights of Cyprus, organised by category.

The location of each particular monument is given in brackets, along with a reference to the pages of the book on which further details about it may be found, where travellers can acquaint themselves both with the monument itself, and with the route they should follow to find it.

Figurine from the Archaeological Museum.

1. MUSEUMS

Archaeological Museums:
- NICOSIA (outside the old town, on Mouseiou Street, see p. 80)
- LIMASSOL (to the north of the Municipal Garden, on Kaningos Street, see p. 109)
- EPISKOPI (on the Limassol-Paphos road, heading west, to the north of the village of Kolossi, see p. 122)
- PAPHOS (in the Upper Town, on Griva Diyeni Street, see p. 145)
- KOUKLIA (in the Lusignan palace at the village of Kouklia, see p. 150)
- LARNACA (Kalogreon Square, see p. 175)
- PIERIDIS MUSEUM (in the old town of Larnaca, on Zinonos Street, see p. 175)

Byzantine Museums:
- NICOSIA (housed in the Makarios III Cultural Centre, see p. 77).
- PAPHOS (housed in the Bishopric in the Upper Town, see p. 145)

Medieval Museums:
- LIMASSOL (housed in the Medieval Castle of Limassol, see p. 106)
- LARNACA (housed in the fort of Larnaca, see p. 175)

Folk Art Museums:
- NICOSIA (housed in the Old Archbishopric, see p. 77)
- GOLD-WORK MUSEUM (near the Popular Quarter, Praxippou Street 7-9, see p. 76)
- LIMASSOL (near Ayiou Andreou Street, see p. 108)
- YEROSKIPOU (on the Paphos-Limassol road, to the east of the town, near Pano Paphos, see p. 146)

MAP OF CHURCHES AND MONASTERIES

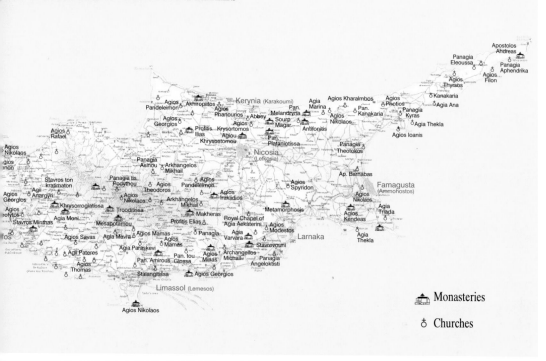

Agii
Anargyri
Agios Rafael
Agios Nikolaos
gios
non
Agios
Georgios
ofytos
Stavros Minthas
OS
Stavros ton
kratimaton
Khrysorrogiatissa
Agia Moni
Mesapotamou
Agios Savas
Agii Pateres
Agios
Thomas
Agia Paraskevi
Agia Mavra
Stalangitissa

Agios
Pandeleimon
Akhiropiitos
Agios
Phariourios
Agios
Georgios
Profitis
Ilias
Khrysostomou
Panagia
Asinou
Panagia tis
Podythou
Agios
Theodoros
Agios
Nikolaos
Arkhangelos
Mikhail
Tro-oditissa
Agios Mamas
Agios
Mamas
Pan. tou
Glossa

Abbey
Krysortomos
Agiou

Arkhangelos
Mikhail
Arkhangelos
Mikhail
Profitis Elias
Panagia
Agia
Varvara
Agios
Minas
Archangellos
Michail
Stalangitissa

Kerynia (Karakoumi)

Pan.
Melandryina
Sourp
Magar

Agia
Marina
Agios Kharalmbos
Agios
Nikolaos

Agios
Photios
Pan.
Kanakaria
Agia Ana
Kanakaria

Antifonitis

Nicosia
(Lefkosia)

Pan
Plataniotissa

Agios
Spyridon

Metamorphosis

Makheras
Royal Chapel of
Agia Aekaterini
Agia
Varvara
Stavrovouni
Agios
Modestos
Agia
Thekla
Panagia
Angeloktisti

Ap. Barnabas

Agios
Nikolaos
Agios
Kendeas

Agia
Triada

Larnaka

Agios Georgios

Limassol (Lemesos)

Panagia
Theotokos

Famagusta
(Ammohostos)

Apostolos
Ahdreas
Panagia
Eleoussa
Panagia
Aphendrika
Agios
Thyrsos
Agios
Filon
Kanakaria
Panagia
Kyras
Agia Thekla
Agios Ioanis

Agios Nikolaos

🏛 Monasteries

⛪ Churches

MAP OF ARCHAEOLOGICAL SITES

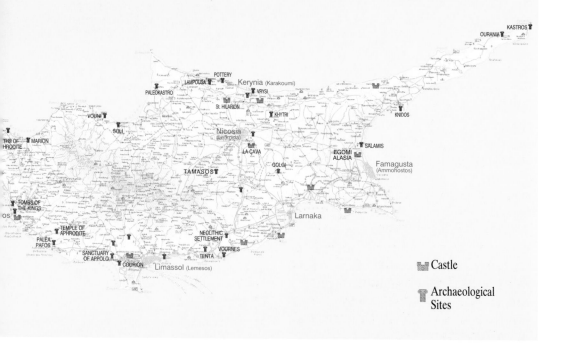

THS OF
HRODITE
MARION

TOMBS OF
THE KINGS
OS
TEMPLE OF
APHRODITE
PALEA
PAFOS
SANCTUARY
OF APPOLO.

VOUNI

SOLI

PALEOKASTRO
LAMPOUSA
POTTERY
VRYSI
St. HILARION
TAMASOS

NEOLITHIC
SETTLEMENT
TENTA
VOURNES
COURION

Kerynia (Karakoumi)

KHYTRI

Nicosia
(Lefkosia)

LA CAVA

GOLGI

Limassol (Lemesos)

KNIDOS

EGOMI
ALASIA

SALAMIS

Famagusta
(Ammohostos)

Larnaka

OURANIA
KASTROS

🏰 Castle

🏛 Archaeological
Sites

61

Other Museums:

- LEVENDIS MUNICIPAL MUSEUM, NICOSIA
  (Ippokratous Street 17, see p. 74)
- MUSEUM OF THE NATIONAL LIBERATION STRUGGLE
  (housed in the Old Archbishopric, see p. 78)
- CYPRUS ETHNOLOGICAL MUSEUM (housed in the old
  mansion of Chatziyorgakis Kornesios, dragoman of
  Cyprus at Patriarchou Grigoriou Street 20, see p. 78)
- ETHNOGRAPHIC MUSEUM OF PAPHOS
  (Exo Vrysis Street, see p. 145)
- MUSEUM OF MARINE LIFE (at Ayia Napa in the
  unoccupied part of the province of Famagusta, see p. 191)

Art Galleries:

- NICOSIA (housed in the Makarios III Cultural Centre,
  see p. 77)

Libraries:

- NICOSIA (housed in the Makarios III Cultural Centre
  (see p. 77)
- LIMASSOL MUNICIPAL LIBRARY
  (Ayiou Andreou Street, see p. 108)

Inside the Museum of Folk Art.

2. CHURCHES

Province of Nicosia:

- Church of Trypiotis (Solonos Street, see p. 76)
- Cathedral of Ayios Ioannis Theologos (in the town of Nicosia,
  between the Old and New Archbishoprics, see p.78)
- Church of the Phaneromeni (in the old town, see p. 79)
- Church of the Panayia Chrysospiliotissa
  (in the old town, see p. 79)
- Church of Peristerona (on the road west of Nicosia, after
  the plain of Morphou, at the village of Peristerona, see p. 82).
- Church of Asinou (on the Nicosia-Troodos road, 20 km.
  North of Kakopetria and 5 km from Nikitari, see p. 83)
- Church of Ayios Sozomenos
  (at the village of Galata, see p. 84)
- Church of Archangelos Michael or the Theotokos
  (at the village of Galata, see p. 84)
- Church of the Panayia Podithou
  (at the village of Galata, see p. 84)
- Church of Ayios Nikolaos tis Stegis
  (5 km. from Kakopetria, see p. 85)
- Church of the Panayia Theotokos
  (5 km. from Kakopetria, see p. 85)
- Church of Ayios Yeoryios Perachoritis
  (5 km. from Kakopetria, see p. 85)
- Church of Ayios Ioannis Lambadistis
  (on the east side of Setrachos, see p. 86)
- Church of the Panayia Mouttoula
  (village of Mouttoulas, see p. 86)
- Church of Archangelos Michael (at Pedoulas, see p. 86)
- Church of the Panayia Chrysospiliotissa
  (11 km. from Nicosia, near the village of Deftera, see p. 93)
- Church of Archangelos Michael (at the village of Pera,
  about 18 km. south-west of Nicosia, see p. 93)
- Church of the Panayia Odigitria (at the village of Pera,
  about 18 km. south-west of Nicosia, see p. 93)
- Church of the Metamorphosis (at the village of Palaichori,
  45 km. south of Nicosia, see p. 97)
- Church of the Chrysopantanassa (at the village of
  Palaichori, 45 km. south of Nicosia, see p. 97)
- Church of the Panayia Eleousa (at the village of Agros,
  57 km. from Nicosia and 39 km. from Limassol, see p. 97)
- Church of the Timios Stavros (at Platanistasa, see p. 98)
- Church of the Panayia Araka (at Lagoudera, see p. 98)
- Church of Ayios Eftychios (at Pera Chora, a few km.
  from Nicosia, see p. 99)

Province of Limassol:

- Church of Ayia Napa (in the old town of Limassol,
  on Ayiou Andreou Street, see p. 106)
- Church of the Panayia Eleousa
  (near the village of Trimiklini, see p. 111)
- Church of the Timios Stavros (at Pelendri, see p. 118)
- Church of the Panayia Katholiki (at Pelendri, see p. 118)
- Church of the Chysospiliotissa
  (at the village of Kandou, see p. 117)
- Church of Ayia Marina
  (at the village of Kandou, see p. 118)
- Church of Ayia Mavra (at the village of Kilani, see p. 118)

The church of the Panayia Theoskepasti of Paphos.

Province of Paphos:
- Catacomb of Ayia Solomoni (town of Paphos, see p. 140)
- Church of the Panayia Limeniotisssa
  (near the harbour of Paphos, see p. 143)
- Church of Ayia Kyriaki Chrysospiliotissa
  (in the centre of Lower Paphos, see p. 144)
- Church of the Panayia Theoskepasti
  (100 m. east of Ayia Kyriaki, see p. 145)
- Church of Ayia Paraskevi (Yeroskipou, see p. 146)
- Church of the Panayia Chryseleousa
  (village of Emba, see p. 154)
- Church of the Panayia Chryseleousa (Polemi, see p. 155)

Province of Larnaca:
- Church of Ayios Lazaros (on the coastal road,
  in the centre of the town, see p. 175)
- Church of the Panayia Angeloktisti
  (village of Kiti, see p. 178)

Unoccupied area of Famagusta:
- Church and monastery of Ayia Napa
  (at Ayia Napa, 40 km. east of Larnaca, see p. 188)
- Church of Ayios Yeoryios (at Derynia, see p. 196)
- Church of Ayia Marina (at Derynia, see p. 196)
- Church of the Panayia (at Derynia, see p. 196)
- Church of Ayios Mamas (at Sotira, see p. 196)
- Church of the Panayia Chardakiotissa
  (1 km. west of Sotira, see p. 196)
- Church of Ayios Andronikos (Frenaros, see p. 196)
- Church of Archangelos Michael (Frenaros, see p. 196)
- Church of the Panayia Eleousa
  (at Liopetri, 14 km. north-west of Ayia Napa, see p. 196)
- Church of Ayios Yeoryios Teratsiotis
  (at Avgorou, 19 km. north-west of Ayia Napa, see p. 196)

Occupied Cyprus:
- Cathedral of Ayia Sophia (Nicosia, see p. 207)
- Church of Ayios Nikolaos (at Famagusta, see p. 203)
- Church of the Panayia Kanakaria (Lythrankomi, see p. 206)
- Abbey of Bellapais (at the village of Bellapais, north of the
  Pentadaktylos range, see p. 212)

3. MONASTERIES
Province of Nicosia:
- Kykkou Monastery (on the west side of the Marathasa plain,
  13 km. west of Pedoulas, see p. 90)
- Monastery of Ayios Iraklidios (Politiko, see p. 94)
- Monastery of Macheras (south of Politiko, see p. 95)

Province of Limassol:
- Monastery of the Trooditissa (Platres, see p. 114)

Province of Paphos:
- Monastery of Ayios Neophytos , (see p. 162)

Province of Larnaca:
- Monastery of Stavrovouni (Larnaca - Limassol, see p. 179)
- Monastery of Ayia Varvara (Stavrovouni, see p. 180)
- Monastery of Ayios Minas (east of Vavla, see p. 182)

Unoccupied area of Famagusta:
- Monastery of Ayios Kendeas (north of Avgorou, see p. 196)

Occupied Cyprus:
- Monastery of Apostolos Varnavas (Enkomi, see p. 302)
- Monastery of Ayios Andreas (on the Karpasia peninsula)
- Monastery of Ayios Ioannis Chrysostomos (Kyrenia, see p. 216)
- Monastery of Ayios Panteleimon (at Myrtou, see p. 215)
- Monastery of Ayios Mamas (at Morphou, see p. 216)

View of Ayia Napa.

4. ARCHAEOLOGICAL SITES

Province of Nicosia:
- Tamasos (near the village of Politiko, south-west of Nicosia, see p. 94)

Province of Limassol:
- Amathus (near the town sea-front, see p. 109)
- Kourion (on the Limassol-Paphos road to the west, see p. 125)
- Ancient theatre (south of the archaeological site of Kourion, see p. 126)
- Early Christian basilica (Kourion, see p. 128)
- Roman agora - Nymphaeum (near the Early Christian basilica, see p. 128)
- Kourion stadium (2 km. from Kourion, see p. 128)
- Sanctuary of Apollo Hylates (4 km. from Kourion, see p. 129)

Province of Paphos:
- Tombs of the Kings (1 km. north-west of the harbour of Paphos, see p. 140)
- Paphos Odeion (near the Lighthouse, see p. 143)
- Agora (in front of the Paphos odeion, see p. 143)
- Asklepieion (south of the Roman odeion, see p. 143)
- Saranda Kolones (on a hill to the right of the main road, see p. 143)
- Palaipaphos (on the Paphos - Limassol road to the east of the town, see p. 146)

Province of Larnaca:
- Kamares (on the Larnaca - Limassol road, see p. 175)
- Chirokitia (near Tochni, see p. 182)
- Tenda (near Kalavasos, see p. 182)

Occupied Cyprus:
- Enkomi (east coast of Cyprus, see p. 205)
- Ancient Salamis (near Famagusta, see p. 204)
- Ancient city of Soloi (see p. 217)
- Vouni (near Soloi, see p. 217)

1. View of Kourion.
2. Tombs of the Kings at Paphos.

5. CASTLES

Province of Nicosia:
- Venetian fortifications (in the old town of Nicosia, see p. 74)

Province of Limassol:
- Medieval castle (near the old harbour of Limassol, see p. 106)
- Medieval castle of Kolossi (on the Limassol - Paphos road, to the west, see p. 122)

Province of Paphos:
- Medieval fortress of Paphos (in the small harbour of Lower Paphos, see p. 144)
- Medieval palace of the Lusignans (Kouklia, see p. 150)

Province of Larnaca:
- Fortress of Larnaca (on the coast road, see p. 175)

Occupied Cyprus:
- Tower of Othello (at Famagusta, see p. 205)
- Kyrenia castle (on the east side of the harbour, see p. 210)
- Castle of St. Hilarion (in the foothills of the Pentadaktylos range, see p. 211)
- Castle of Buffavento (at a height of 954 m. in the Pentadaktylos range)
- Castle of Kantara (built on one of the easternmost peaks of Pentadaktylos, see p. 212)

6. MOSAICS

Province of Limassol:
- House of Eustolios (near the ancient theatre of Kourion, see p. 127)
- House of the Gladiators (near Kourion, see p. 127)
- House of Achilles (at the north entrance to Kourion, see p. 127)

Province of Paphos:
- House of Dionysos (near the harbour of Paphos, see p. 141)
- House of Theseus (in the same area, see p. 142)
- House of Aion (in the same area, see p. 142)
- House of Orpheus (west of the House of Theseus, see p. 142)

7. BEAUTY SPOTS

Province of Limassol:
- Kalidonia waterfalls (at Platres, see p. 112)
- Nature trails: Artemis, Atalanta, Aidonia, Persephone, on the summit of Troodos, see p. 114)

Province of Paphos:
- Petra tou Romiou (on the Paphos - Limassol road, see p. 150)
- Baths of Aphrodite (a few km. from Latsi, see p. 157)
- Akamas (on the peninsula in the north-west of Cyprus, see p. 158)
- Gorge of Avakas (starts at Koloni, see p. 160)

Province of Larnaca:
- Salt-lakes (near the international airport, see p. 176)

1. The castle at Paphos.
2. Mosaic from Paphos.
3. Enchanting sunset at Paphos.

TOUR OF CYPRUS

The beautiful island of Cyprus captivates visitors at first sight, with its notable historical monuments, picturesque little villages, intricately indented coasts, and superb mountain sites. To enable visitors to make the best use of the time available to them and enjoy this beautiful land, we have divided the island into six areas: the provinces of **Nicosia, Limassol, Paphos** and **Larnaca, the unoccupied area of Famagusta,** and **Occupied Cyprus**.

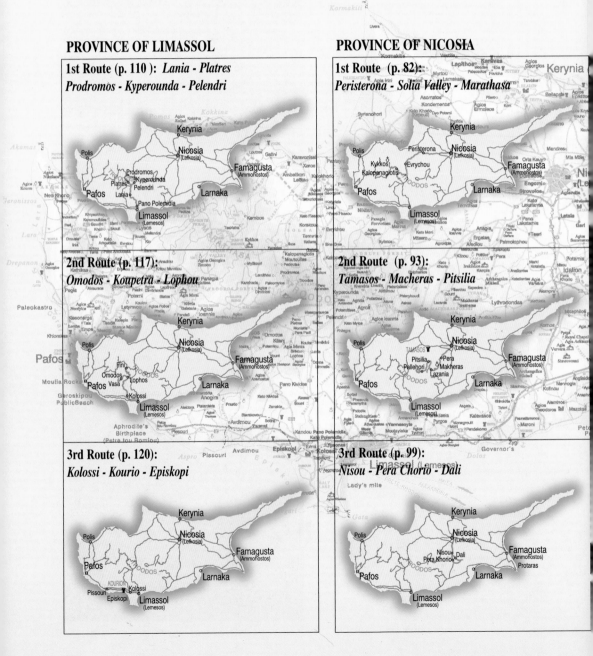

PROVINCE OF LIMASSOL

1st Route (p. 110): *Lania - Platres Prodromos - Kyperounda - Pelendri*

2nd Route (p. 117): *Omodos - Koupetra - Lophou*

3rd Route (p. 120): *Kolossi - Kourio - Episkopi*

PROVINCE OF NICOSIA

1st Route (p. 82): *Peristerona - Solia Valley - Marathasa*

2nd Route (p. 93): *Tamasos - Macheras - Pitsilia*

3rd Route (p. 99): *Nisou - Pera Chorio - Dali*

PROVINCE OF LARNACA (p. 176)

Lefkara - Chirokitia - Dekelia

OCCUPIED CYPRUS (p. 198)

UNOCCUPIED FAMAGUSTA (p. 186)

Ayia Napa - Paralimni - Protaras - Derynia
Sotira - Frenaros - Liopetri

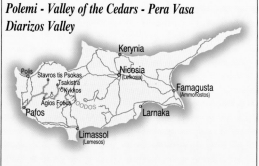

PROVINCE OF PAPHOS

1st Route (p. 146):
Yeroskipou - Palaipaphos - Petra tou Romiou

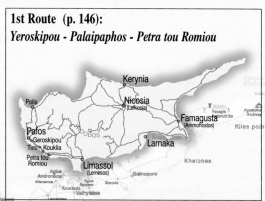

2nd Route (p. 154):
Coral Bay - Latsi - Baths of Aphrodite - Akamas

3rd Route (p. 162):
Monastery of Ayios Neophytos - Chrysochou - Pyrgos

4th Route (p. 164):
Polemi - Valley of the Cedars - Pera Vasa
Diarizos Valley

6

PROVINCE OF NICOSIA
The town and routes in the surrounding area

*Memories of the past come to life
in many parts of the town.*

The province of Nicosia is in the centre of the island, and borders with all the other provinces, while a small area of it in the north marches with the sea. This is the region of Morphou and Tillyria, which is now occupied by the Turks.

The province includes about 30% of the total area of the island and has a population of 245,000. Most of it consists of plain, though the west and south parts towards the Troodos range are mountainous or hilly, with a number of valleys. Large tracts of the province that are not irrigated are devoted to the cultivation of corn and other cereals, while the irrigated areas and valleys produce citrus and other fruit, and vegetables. About 47% of the industrial units of Cyprus are located in the province of Nicosia, where they are concentrated in industrial zones in the area around the capital. Although tourism in Cyprus is focused on the coasts, there are several hotels in the city of Nicosia, and the mountain resorts in the province have some excellent agro-tourist accommodation. To get to know this region, visitors may first tour the town and then visit the areas around it by road. To assist in this, we have devised three routes. The first route takes us towards the north side of the Troodos range, where we explore the west and south-west part of the province, visiting Peristerona and the picturesque villages in the Solia and Marathasa valleys.

The second route takes us to the south part of the province and the villages of Deftera, Pera, and Politiko, and the area to the east of Mount Olympos, which is known as Pitsilia.

Finally, the third route follows the national highway from Nicosia to Limassol, and allows visitors to explore the areas to the south and south-east of the capital.

Nicosia

The town of Nicosia lies in the middle of the central plain of Cyprus. It has been the largest town, and the capital of the island since the Middle Ages, with a present population of about 177,000 inhabitants.

Finds dating from the Chalcolithic period have been discovered in the area of Prodromos, on the left bank of the river Pedieos, near the site of modern Nicosia. During the Early Bronze Age, when Cyprus was prospering from its output of copper, three settlements were founded in the surrounding area of Nicosia. The main factors in the inhabitation of this area were the water-supply from the river Pedieos and the fertility of the soil, which favoured the development of farming and stock-raising. At present there is no clear evidence for the continued occupation of the area after the Early Bronze Age, but Ledra is mentioned in the 7th c. BC, when there is reference to Onasagoras, king of Ledra. (Down to Byzantine times, Nicosia was known by its original name of Ledra).

In Roman times, Ledra was a small, insignificant rural settlement. During the period of the Arab raids, many of the inhabitants of coastal settlements moved to the interior of the island. After this, in the Byzantine period, Nicosia became the capital of the island.

During the Frankish period, Nicosia became the administrative centre of the island; imposing buildings and churches were erected, and the kings were crowned here. Under the Lusignans the first fortifications were constructed. These were followed by others built by the Venetians when they were masters of the island; these latter fortifications had a smaller perimeter, so that they would be some distance from the surrounding hills.

Entrance to the town was by way of three gates: the Kyrenia, Paphos and Famagusta gates. The Venetians also built an artificial canal to channel the waters of the Pedieos outside the town.

Under Turkish domination, Nicosia continued to be the capital of the island. This was a period of economic and cultural decline, when many of the Frankish churches were converted into mosques.

During the period of British rule, the Presidential Residence was erected of timber on the site it still occupies. It was at this time that the town began to spread outside the walls. The road network was also extended, and linked Nicosia with other parts of the island. This development led to an increase in the population of Nicosia. There was a further increase after the declaration of the independence of Cyprus in 1960; this was the consequence of the general movement to the towns, and the concentrating in Nicosia of economic, administrative, cultural and other activities.

LEGEND

1. French Embassy
2. German Embassy
3. U. S. Embassy
4. Russian Embassy
5. Presidential Residence
6. Archibishop's Residence
7. Town Hall
8. Municipal Theatre
9. Police Station
10. General Hospital
11. Cyprus Museum
12. Phaneromeni Library
13. Makarios Cultural Centre
14. Museum of the National Liberation Struggle
15. Museum of Folk Art
16. Nicosia Cultural Centre
17. Chatziyorgakis Mansion
18. Centre for Cypriot Art
19. Municipal Library
20. National Collection of Modern Art
21. Municipal Market
22. Telephone Office
23. Tourist Information Office
24. Cyprus Airways
25. Mosque
26. Byzantine Museum
27. National Art Gallery
28. Post Office
29. Greek Embassy
30. Pancypriot High School
31. Monument to Liberty
32. Eleftherias Square
33. Stadium
34. Swimming pool

SAIXPIR

SPYROU CHRISTODOULOU

DAMONOS

AGIOU DITRIOU

SAIOU NAPOLEONTOS

NORMAN

SAVVA ROTSIDI

IROON

AVEROF

MARKOU DRAKOU

KYRINIAS

LYSIPPOU

AEGEOS

KOMPTON MAKENZI

Agios Georgios ⚥

IOU PAVLOU

PAPHOU

Agios Kassianos ⚥

LEOPHOROS P. KAPOTA

SOLONOS MICHAILI

Panagia Chrysaliniotissa ⚥

DIMONAKTOS

Timiou
Stavrou ⚥

EKTOROS

ERMOU

JOHN KENNE

UKI AKRITA

KINYRA

LEDRAS

AMMOCHOSTOU

16

SALAMINOS

LARNAKA

ZANNETOU

MESOLONGIOU

KATALANOU

MAR MOUSKOU

ARSINOIS

27

14

26

Agios Ioannis ⚥

21

Faneromeni ⚥

15

31

8

MOUSIOU

9

13

32

PROTAGOROU

IMVROU

DELFON

ACHEON

11

AEGYPTOU

Agios
Savvas ⚥

17

TRIKOUPI

AGIOU ANDONIOU

PROTA GOROU

VOLONAKI

ROIKOU

GREVENOU

THIVON

MARKOU

LEOPHOROS OMIROU

10

12

AREOS

25

DIGENI AKRITA

VAS. AMALIAS

METOKHIOU

KHILONOS

ILIOUPOLEOS

18

23

STASINOU

KALLIPOLEOS

SINA

PRODROMOU

30

Agios Pavlos ⚥

7

29

33

PINDAROU

KLIMENTOS

ANDRIA

THESSALIAS

3

PLOUTARCHOU

VASILEOS PAVLOU

19

28

STASANDROU

KRITIS

KYPRIANDROS

ANDROKLEOUS

KALAVRYTON

DIMITSANIS

GLADSTONE

34

STASIKRATOUS

LEOPHOROS ARCHIEPISKOPOU MAKARIOU III

NAXOU

ORFEOS

1

VASILI MICHAILIDI

AGION OMOLOGIT

MENANDROU

ETHNIKIS FROURAS

GEORGIOU GRIVA DIGENI

20

35

THEMISTOKLI

FLORINIS

⚥ AGAPINOROS

KARPENISIOU

LEOFHOROS EVAGOROU

G.HANTZIDAKI

MINASIADOU

NIKOREONDOS

ANDREA MICHALAKOPOULOU

KREONTOS

VYZANTIOU

PRODROMOU

SANTA ROSA

GERAS

MOLDAMOFONTOS

ZINONOS

PENTE PIGADIA

AGLANGIAS

LEFKONOS

DIMITRIOU SEVERI

RODOU

ATHO

SAMOU

CHIOU

AKAMANTOS

A. ARAOUZOU

KARPENISIOU

2

LEOPHOROS KENNEDY

5

KYRIAKOU MATSI

IKAROU

GLAFKOU

KASOU

MARTIOU 25

ESTIAS

ELEFTHEROUPOLEOS

NIKIS

RIGA FEREOU

ESPERIDON

ARSINOIS

LEOFOROS LEMESSOU

ARSINOIS

STASINOU

SANS SOUSI

THOUKIDIDOU

KIMONOS

ARMENIAS

IPPOKRATOUS

Agios
Dimitrios ⚥

IFIGENIAS

KALYPSOUS

PROEDRIKOU MEGAROU

LEONIDOU

THERMOPYLON

KERYNIAS

KOLOKOTRONI

KORYTSAS

MESOLONGIOU

KERYNIAS

ARISTOKYPROU

CHRYSANTHOU M.

PRODROMOU

OKTOVRIOU 28

LEOFOROS AKROPOLEOS

ARCH. KYPRIANOU

AGIAS MARINAS

SOULIOU

ACHILLEOS

RIK

AKADIMIAS

THISEOS

STROVOLOU

PERIKLEOUS

ATHALASSIS AVENUE

DASOUPOLEOS

ANDREA DIDMITRIOU ⚥

KONSTANTINOU K.

KOSTI PALAMA

Tour of the Town

Since the Turkish invasion in 1974, Nicosia has been divided into two. In recent years unoccupied Nicosia has developed in leaps and bounds. It consists of a new and an old town, harmoniously combined in a beautiful whole.

The **new town**, which spreads around the old, consists of a large number of neighbourhoods. It is a cosmopolitan town with wide streets, modern shops, banks, hotels, squares and fine residences. It is the headquarters of the public services and all the foreign embassies. The town lives and moves to European rhythms. In recent years it has established itself as the ideal Middle East centre for international conferences, with an excellent system of telecommunications.

The **old town** is enclosed within the famous Venetian walls built in the 16th c., which are the most characteristic monument of the capital. Designed by the Venetian architect Giulio Savorgnano and erected between 1567 and 1570, they are the most majestic monument in the capital. They are 4.5 km. in length and have eleven heart-shaped bastions. There are only three gates: in the north (Kyrenia Gate), east (Famagusta Gate) and west (Paphos Gate). The east, or Famagusta Gate (porta Giuliana) has been restored and is used as a cultural centre by the Municipality of Nicosia. It consists of a large vaulted passage with two side rooms. The internal entrance is particularly imposing, while the outer one opens cn to the moat that surrounds the walls. In 1984 it was awarded the Europa Nostra prize for its exemplary conservation and conversion into a living cultural centre.

Our tour of the old town, with its narrow, labyrinthine streets and neighbourhoods, starts from Eleftherias Square, which is situated between the old town and the modern town that evolved after the 19th c. Here stands the Town Hall, in one of the bastions of the Venetian fortifications, called the D'Avila bastion. A few metres to the west are the two busiest shopping streets,

Lidras Street and Onasagorou Street, which is parallel with it. This was once the main shopping centre of the capital.

Leaving Eleftherias Square opposite the main post-office in Nicosia and turning left into a little street, we come to the Laiki Yeitonia (popular quarter). This is a small paved area that recalls the atmosphere of the old days. It has traditional buildings dating from the 19th and early 20th c., some of which have been restored, while the architecture of some of the others still retains the character of the period. If we wish to learn more of the history of Nicosia, we may visit the:

Levendis Municipal Museum

This is a restored, two-storey, 19th c. building at Ippokratous Street 17, near the Laiki Yeitonia, devoted to the history of the capital over the centuries. It houses a display of photographs, engravings, a list of governors and officials of Cyprus, details of the heavy taxes imposed by the Ottoman Turks, dragomans, Venetian coins, Byzantine icons and many other items.

Close to the Laiki Yeitonia, at Praxippou Street 7-9, is the:

1. Narrow street in the popular quarter.
2. Famagusta Gate.
3, 4. Views of the old town.

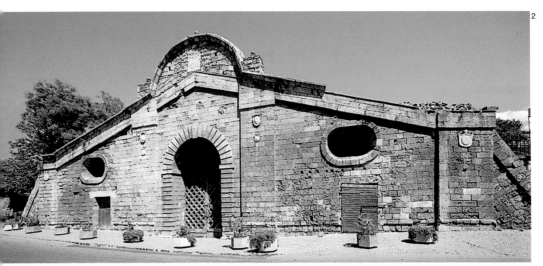

Museum of Gold-work

This museum contains examples of the goldsmith's art from the late 19th-20th c., consisting of jewellery, sacred vessels and old tools.

Continuing along Solonos Street in this same neighbourhood, we come to the church of Trypiotis, built in 1695, which is a fine example of a Frankish-Byzantine church.

Leaving behind the Laiki Yeitonia, our stroll in the streets of the old town is a return to the past. The narrow streets, culs-de-sac, old archontika ("mansions") with their balconies, carved out of the yellowish stone of Nicosia, and the little old workshops, where the craftsmen continue to practise their art, all exude an atmosphere of nostalgia. The notorious Green Line of Cyprus, which divides the capital in two, runs through here, and many of the narrow alleys are abruptly interrupted by the confrontation line. Guardposts flying the national flags can be seen on either side.

Although this zone is densely built, it is not very densely occupied. Near the Green Line most of the houses are in a wretched condition, almost on the point of collapse. Those of the owners who had the choice decided to abandon them. In some of the two-storey buildings, the upper storey is in poor condition, with broken shutters and gaping roofs, while the ground floor is occupied by workshops or shops. The municipal authorities are making efforts to improve the use of this area. In many cases, these old houses are being converted and house expensive restaurants or bars.

A few steps from the Laiki Yeitonia we come to Arch. Kyprianou Square, and the:

Archbishop's Residence

This is a striking two-storey building in a neo-Byzantine style, constructed of yellowish stone. It was erected in 1956-1960 and is the residence of the archbishop of Cyprus, and seat of the Cypriot Greek Orthodox Church. It houses a large number of icons, manuscripts and other treasures of the Cypriot church. In front of this building, a colossal bronze statue of Archbishop Makarios III was erected in 1987; Makarios was the first president of the Republic of Cyprus (1960-1977) and archbishop of Cyprus from 1950 to his death in 1977. The monument is the work of the Cypriot sculptor N. Kotzamanis. On the other side of the building is a bust of Archbishop Kyprianos, who was hanged by the Turks in 1821.

*The Archbishop's Residence
with the statue of Makarios.*

Makarios III Cultural Centre

This comprises the Byzantine Museum, the Art Gallery, and the Library.

The **Byzantine Museum** has an impressive collection of 150 Byzantine portable icons from churches and monasteries all over Cyprus, dating from the 8th to the 18th c. This gives visitors the chance to trace the development of Cypriot religious art and the various techniques used from time to time. The museum is considered one of the finest of its kind in the world.

In the east wing of the Archbishop's residence is the **Library** of the Archbishop Makarios III Cultural Foundation. The art collections on the ground floor include oil paintings, maps, drawings and other works of historical interest. The upper floor houses works by European artists who were inspired by Greek history, especially the Greek War of Independence of 1821.

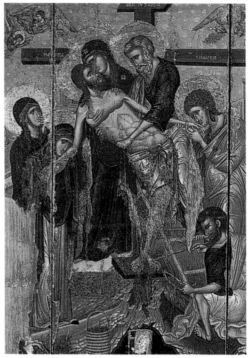

Icon of the Descent from the Cross, from the church of Ayia Marina at Kalopanayiotis. Byzantine Museum in the Makarios III Cultural Centre.

It is worth visiting the Byzantine Museum to admire the excellent examples of Cypriot religious painting. The mosaics of the Virgin Kanakaria are of particular interest: they were illegally sold abroad by the Turks and were recently returned to Cyprus after a successful law suit.

The Old Archbishopric building, near the new Archbishop's Residence, houses the:

Museum of Folk Art

This contains a collection of Cypriot folk art of the 19th and early 20th c. Woodcarvings, handicrafts and embroideries, pottery, Cypriot costumes, and loom-woven fabrics are on display for visitors to admire. In the same building is the:

Church of Ayios Ioannis Theologos.

Museum of the National Liberation Struggle

This museum was created in 1961, one year after the proclamation of the independence of Cyprus. It contains souvenirs (documents, photographs, personal items of freedom fighters, letters, etc.) relating to the liberation struggle against the British from 1955 to 1959.

In the area between the old and new Archbishop Residences stands the **cathedral of Ayios Ioannis Theologos**, which was built in 1662 on the ruins of an earlier medieval church. Visitors are dazzled by the well-preserved wall-paintings and the wood-carved iconostasis. The 18th c. wall-paintings, the work of Archbishop Philotheos, depict scenes from the Holy Scriptures, as well as the discovery of the tomb of St. Barnabas at Salamis and the subsequent recognition of the church of Cyprus as autocephalous by the emperor Zeno.

In Arch. Kyprianou Square, opposite the buildings just described, is the:

Pancypriot High School

The oldest and most historic secondary-level educational institution on Cyprus, this was founded in 1812 by Archbishop Kyprianos, and is still functioning. In 1896 it was recognised as equal in status to the six-grade high schools of Greece, and it was at this time that it received its present name. After visiting these sights, we may proceed 200 m. to the south-west of the Archbishop's Residence, to Patriarchou Grigoriou Street 20, where we find an impressive old archontiko ("mansion"). This is **the house of the dragoman of Cyprus, Chatziyorgakis Kornesios**. A fine house and a notable example of 18th c. urban architecture, it now houses the Cyprus Ethnological Museum, which was awarded the Europa Nostra prize in 1988.

Proceeding 200 m. eastward from the Archbishop's residence, we come to the Monument to Liberty, which stands on a bastion in the Venetian fortifications known as the Podocataro bastion.

Monument to Liberty.

Iconostasis in the church of Ayios Ioannis Theologos.

The inspiration and creation of Notaras, it is highly impressive in terms of its overall composition and details. The monument was erected in 1970, ten years after the proclamation of the independence of Cyprus, and commemorates the liberation struggle (1955-1959) of the Cypriots against the British. It depicts Liberty as a woman standing at the highest point of the monument and looking down at two soldiers who are opening the prison gates, so that 14 figures, representing all the types of people to be found on the island, can emerge from the darkness into the light. To the left of the Monument of Liberty, we come to the **Famagusta Gate**. Inside the old town, we should not fail to visit the churches of the Phaneromeni, the Panayia Chrysaliniotissa, Ayios Antonios and Ayios Kassianos. The **Church of the Phaneromeni** in the old town of Nicosia was built in 1872 in a Frankish-Byzantine style and is the largest church within the fortifications. To the east of it is a mausoleum containing the remains of Archbishop Kyprianos and other clergymen hanged by the Turks in 1821.

The **Church of the Chrysaliniotissa** is thought to be the earliest Byzantine church in Nicosia. Built in 1450 by Eleni Palaiologos, wife of the Lusignan king John I, it stands on the ruins of an earlier church of unknown date. It houses a collection of rare icons of Byzantine times, and a further 25 icons are housed in the Byzantine Museum of Nicosia. In Trikoupi Street, near the market of the old Town Hall, we come to Omerye Mosque. This was formerly a church of the Augustinian monks dedicated to St. Marina. It was built in 1571, and after the capture of Nicosia by the Turks, was converted into a mosque by Mustafa Pasha, who asserted that the prophet Omer rested in this place when he visited Nicosia. Outside the walls, at the junction of Stasinou Avenue and Kritis Street, we may visit the **National Collection of Modern Art**. This is housed in a neoclassical building and contains a collection of paintings and sculpture by 70 Cypriot artists.

Archaeological Museum of Nicosia

This is the largest and most important archaeological museum on Cyprus. It was founded in 1908 and houses the cultural heritage of 9000 years, with representative items dating from the Neolithic period to Early Byzantine times. In the 14 rooms of the museum, visitors may follow the historical evolution of art on Cyprus (pottery, sculpture and architecture). The first three rooms are devoted to artefacts of the Neolithic period with incised and relief decoration (figurines, pottery), followed by Mycenaean vases dating from the 15th c. BC and pottery of the Cypro-Geometric, Cypro-Archaic and Cypro-Classical periods. The evolution of sculpture may be traced through the collection of 2000 terracotta figurines from the temple at Ayia Irini (700 BC) and through statues dating from the 7th c. BC to Roman times (kouroi, statue of Zeus Keraunios, head of Aphrodite, bronze statue of Septimius Severus, and the charming statue of a sleeping Eros).

In the other rooms of the museum are to be found collections of helmets and weapons, the famous mosaic "emblem" from Palaipaphos, and extensive collections of jewellery and coins. There is an interesting room with a reconstruction of burial customs, and another in which the history of writing on Cyprus is presented through inscriptions. Directly opposite the museum is the:

Municipal Theatre of Nicosia

A modern building erected in 1967, the theatre has a capacity of 1200. Its stage is used for performances of plays, recitals, concerts and cultural events of all kinds. In this same area stands the building of the **House of Representatives**, the **General Hospital of Nicosia**, and the **Municipal Garden**, a small oasis in the centre of the city. Visitors should not fail to visit two other sites in Nicosia that are directly linked with the recent history of the island: the "Phylakismena Mnimata" and the Makedonitissa Tumulus.

Gold royal sceptre (fig1) and
Statue of Zeus Keraunios (fig2),
Archaeological Museum of Nicosia.

The **"Phylakismena Mnimata"** are in a room in the main prison of Nicosia, in which the bodies are buried of nine of the heroes who were hanged during the 1955-59 liberation struggle, and four who were killed during it. After the end of the struggle, the room was turned into a place of pilgrimage and called the Phylakismena Mnimata (Imprisoned Tombs) The thirteen tombs of the heroes are to the right of the entrance, while to the left are the cells occupied by the condemned men and the gallows on which the British executed the nine heroes.

The **Makedonitissa Tumulus** is in the area of Makedonitissa, 3 km. to the west of Nicosia, near the monastery of the Panayia Makedonitissa. It is a military cemetery and heroon in which are interred Greek and Greek-Cypriot soldiers who fell defending Cyprus in the summer of 1974. The Cyprus International Trade Fair is also held annually on a site of 270,000 square m. at Makedonitissa. The site is equipped with modern stands, recreation areas and other facilities. The exhibitors at the trade fair include many foreign as well as Cypriot industrialists and merchants, and it is held every year at the end of May - beginning of June, attracting thousands of local and foreign visitors.

Finally, to the south of Nicosia in the suburb of Strovolos, is the Presidential Residence. The original building, which was the residence of the British Governor, was a timber structure that was destroyed in October 1931 by Cypriot protestors, during the uprising against the British colonialists known as the "October incident". The building was reconstructed in 1933. It was an impressive edifice with characteristic architecture. Since the acquisition of independence in 1961 it has been the residence of the president of the Republic of Cyprus. During the coup of 1974, it was completely destroyed, apart from the facade, with the British emblem, and a few walls. The building was reconstructed once more to its former design.

Gold and ivory mirror-handle (fig.3)
and Statue of Septimius Severus (fig. 4),
Archaeological Museum of Nicosia.

1st ROUTE:

Peristerona - Solia Valley Marathasa

Leaving the town of Nicosia behind visitors may follow the first route suggested above, which takes in the areas in the west and south-west part of the province. Crossing part of the fertile plain to the west of the city, we ascend the north slopes of the Troodos range by way of the verdant valleys of Solia and Marathasa. This gives us the opportunity to get to know the picturesque mountain villages of Cyprus, with their dry, healthy climate, abundant water, and fruit trees, and above all with their notable Byzantine art and tradition. The large number of churches and monasteries in the region say much of the boundless piety and artistic proclivities of former generations.

Taking the road west of Nicosia towards Troodos, we cross the fertile plain of Morphou, where the different crops cultivated give the landscape a unique atmosphere, particularly in the spring; in the summer, when there is normally no rainfall, it has a drier, almost monotonous aspect. On the road, we come to **Peristerona**, which has a five-domed church of the same name that is of great architectural value. Built in the 11th c., it is a three-aisled Byzantine church dedicated to Saints Barnabas and Hilarion, and the interior was probably covered with wall-painted decoration. The narthex is a later addition, and the renovated iconostasis dates from AD 1549. The church owns several valuable heirlooms, such as two 15th c. patens and a variety of ecclesiastical books, including a gospel book printed in Venice in 1604.

Three-aisled Byzantine church dedicated to SS Barnabas and Hilarion.

The village of Peristerona lies on the left bank of the river of the same name. Visitors are often struck by the fact that a Moslem house of worship stands directly opposite the Christian church of Peristerona - not the only example of this kind of coexistence on Cyprus. This circumstance attests to the fact that before 1974, Greek-Cypriots and Turkish Cypriots lived together peacefully.

Leaving Peristerona, we continue along the Nicosia-Troodos road towards the village of Nikitari, 5 km. outside which we come to the **church of Asinou**, a veritable museum of Byzantine art. The wall-paintings in it date from the 12th to the 17th c. and, coming as they do from different periods, give a vivid picture of the art of Byzantine Cyprus. The small church dating from the late 12th c. was decorated with wall-paintings of the period of the Komnini by painters from Constantinople, in 1105-1106. The church has been described as an "Art Gallery of incalculable value", and is included in the UNESCO list of the World Cultural Heritage.

Our next destination is the **Solia valley**, a tranquil, verdant valley that extends languidly towards the summit of Troodos. Visitors may enjoy the natural beauty of a number of villages, the most important of which are Evrychou, Galata, and Kakopetria, the last more geared to tourism, and also discover small backwaters of Cyprus where time seems to have stood still, where Byzantine art and tradition are still alive.

Evrychou, in the middle of the valley, is a verdant village with extensive irrigated crops of citrus fruits, olives and vegetables.

1. Exterior view of the church of Asinou.
2, 3. Wall-paintings inside the church.

This village was the terminus of the now defunct railway network of Cyprus, which started in Famagusta and passed through Nicosia on its way here. The buildings of the old railway station are still preserved in Evrychou. Some of the Public Services are now centred on this village, and it is the temporary seat of the Bishop of occupied Morphou.

After Evrychou, the Solia valley widens, and as we ascend towards Troodos we come to **Galata,** a village with traditional architecture that is renowned for its Byzantine churches. There are four churches decorated with wall-paintings in and around the village. The **church of Ayios Sozomenos** (early 16th c.), which has a complete ensemble of wall-paintings in a post-Byzantine style, stands in the centre of the village.

The **church of the Archangelos Michael, or Theotokos**, is a small timber-roofed church just below the village, painted in the post-Byzantine style of the 16th c. The church of the **Panayia Podithou**, which belonged to a monastery, was built in 1502, and its wall-paintings are of the Italo-Byzantine style that evolved on Cyprus towards the end of the 15th c., after the conquest of the island by the Venetians (1489). It is included in the UNESCO list of the World Cultural Heritage.

Kakopetria is the most mountainous but also the most visited of the villages in the Solia valley. It is built on either side of a small river called the Klarios or Kargotis, and has an abundance of water that flows in channels on the right and left of almost all its streets. The mountain-sides around it are given over to viticulture, and in areas that can be irrigated, there are orchards with fruit trees, mainly apples. In the west part of the village is the old settlement of Kakopetria, with its characteristic traditional architecture, narrow alleys, stone houses, and wooden balconies, while the east part of it is a more modern settlement. Near the village is the site of **Platania**, to which many people make excursions every weekend. It is a verdant place with many plane-trees and pines, and its facilities make it an ideal site for excursions.

The church of the Panayia Podithou.

Directly opposite is a trout farm, and just below is the Kakopetria windmill, which stands at a height of 800 m., above the main village square, and functioned from the 18th c. until quite recently. It has now been restored and is a tourist attraction. Nearby is a three-storey building with traditional architecture that is used as a restaurant specialising in trout dishes.

In addition to being a summer resort, however, Kakopetria is well-known for its Byzantine churches with their well-preserved wall-paintings.

The best known of them, the **church of Ayios Nikolaos tis Stegis**, is about 5 km. outside Kakopetria and once belonged to a monastery. It was erected in the 11th c., and in the 12th and 13th c. a second timber roof was added, covering the dome and vaults. This feature gave the church its name (stegi means "roof" in Greek). The church is covered with excellent wall-paintings dating between the 11th and the 17th c., and is considered to be one of the most important Byzantine churches on Cyprus. It is included in the UNESCO list of the World Cultural Heritage. The little 16th c. **church of the Panayia Theotokos** also has half its wall-paintings preserved. The **church of Ayios Yeoryios Perachoritis** at the east of the village still has most of its wall-paintings, which date from the first quarter of the 16th c.

Parallel with the Solia valley on the north slopes of the Troodos range lies the **Marathasa valley**, also known as the "alley of the cherry-trees". To get to it, we follow the route described above, but turn left after the village of Peristerona. Some important villages lie in the valley, through which flows the river Setrachos, amongst them Kalopanayiotis, Pedoulas and Mouttoulas. **Kalopanayiotis** is a typical village of the Marathasa area, built on the west side of the valley of the Setrachos.

1, 2. The traditional village of Kakopetria.
3. The church of Ayios Nikolaos tis Stegis.

It is a mountain village with very little cultivable land. In the lower parts of the valley, where the river water can be used for summer irrigation, small areas of land have been levelled to create orchards and gardens with fruit-trees and vegetables. In 1966 a dam with a capacity of 391,000 cubic m. of water was built; it is used for irrigation and has made a distinct contribution to the development of crops. In addition to its fresh, cool climate and abundant fruit, Kalopanayiotis also has medicinal springs.

The **monastery of Ayios Ioannis Lambadistis** is also famous. It stands on the east bank of the Setrachos, near the medicinal springs. It is no longer used as a monastery, but is simply a complex of buildings dating from different periods. The main buildings are the **church of Ayios Iraklidios** at the south, which dates from the 11th c.; the church of Ayios Ioannis Lambadistis, in the middle, which is probably a 12th c. structure; a shared timber-roofed narthex added on the west side of both these churches, and a 15th c. Catholic chapel at the north.

The entire complex is covered by a second roof. In the church of Ayios Iraklidios, the oldest building of the group, are wall-paintings dating from the 11th c. Some of them depict the triumphant entry of Christ into Jerusalem, the Raising of Lazarus, the Crucifixion, the Sacrifice of Abraham, Christ Pantokrator, and so on. In the church of Ayios Ioannis Lambadistis, which was renovated in the 18th c., is housed the saint's skull. The iconostasis dates from the 16th c. and has some notable portable icons.

The narthex is decorated with wall-paintings of the final Byzantine period, just before 1453, when Constantinople fell to the Turks. According to one of the inscriptions, the painter was a refugee from Constantinople and painted this part of the church just after the fall of the capital. Finally, the Catholic chapel has wall-paintings of 1500, which exhibit strong western influence, and have a depiction of the Akathistos Hymn as their main subject. The church of Ayios Ioannis Lambadistis is included in the UNESCO list of the World Cultural Heritage.

Mouttoulas is a village built on the mountainsides, in which the houses seem to be set one on

From the church of Ayios Ioannis Lambadistis.

top of the other. The architecture is predominantly traditional. The most interesting feature of this village, too, is a Byzantine church - one of the nine in the UNESCO list. This church is the **Panayia Mouttoula**, which stands in the upper part of the village, has a timber, lean-to roof, and was built in 1280. The wall-painted decoration extends to the exterior north wall. The subjects are taken from the life of Christ, the life of the Virgin, and other themes. The colours used are predominantly red and blue.

Pedoulas, another mountain holiday resort, is the third village in the region of Marathasa on the way up to Troodos. It has hotel facilities that are highly popular with summer holiday-makers. Its most interesting feature is the Byzantine **church of the Archangelos Michael**, dating from 1474, which is at the lowest point of the village.

The wall-paintings depict scenes from the New Testament, and other fine representations include: the Resurrection of Christ, the Dormition of the Virgin, the Nativity, the Baptism, the Crucifixion, and others. It is one of the nine Byzantine mountain churches included in the UNESCO list of the World Cultural Heritage. Thirteen km. to the west of Pedoulas is the Kykkou Monastery.

1. The traditional village of Kalopanayotis.
2. The village of Pedoula.

The Kalopanayiotis dam, near the village of this name.

Kalopanayiotis.

Kykkou Monastery

This is the most famous and wealthiest monastery on Cyprus. It is situated on the west side of the Marathasa valley, at a height of 1150 m. above sea level. It was built with the financial assistance of the emperor Alexios Komninos, and is called the Sacred Basilica and Stauropegiac Kykkou Monastery.

(The stauropegiac monasteries of Cyprus are those that are self-governing and fall under the spiritual jurisdiction of the archbishop, irrespective of the province in which they are located).The monastery is famous throughout the Orthodox world, thanks to its icon of the Virgin Mary in the church, which is believed to be one of the three icons of the Virgin painted by the St. Luke the Evangelist while the Virgin was still alive.

1. Icon of the Virgin inside the monastery.
2, 3. Exterior view of the monastery,
       and the interior decoration.

The entrance to the monastery, and the courtyard.

The monastery was founded by the hermit Isaiah, probably at the end of the 11th c., during the reign of Alexios Komninos. According to tradition, the icon of the Virgin came to Cyprus in the following way: on one of his hunting expeditions, the Byzantine governor of Cyprus, Manuel Voutomytis, met the hermit Isaiah, at the place where the monastery now stands. Receiving a less than warm reception, he beat the hermit, shortly after which he became seriously ill. Meanwhile, Isaiah had a vision in which the Virgin exhorted him to ask Voutomytis for his help in having her icon brought from Constantinople to Cyprus. Isaiah did in fact visit Voutomytis, who promised that he would fulfil Isaiah's vision. When he began to make preparations for his journey to Constantinople, he started to recover from his illness. When Voutomytis and Isaiah went to Constantinople, the emperor Alexios refused to allow so sacred a treasure to leave the city. Soon, however, both he and his daughter fell victim to the same illness that had afflicted Voutomytis. In the end, Alexios agreed to hand over the icon in order to save his daughter, whereupon both he and his daughter were immediately cured.

The icon was brought to Cyprus amid great pomp, accompanied by the emperor's galley. At the same time, Alexios made a large sum available for the founding of a monastery to house the icon. Despite the fact that the monastery has been burned on several occasions, the miraculous icon has survived. It is considered sacred, and was silvered in 1576. The monastery has recently been restored. The three-aisled church is decorated with wall-paintings near the impressive iconostasis, and wall-paintings also adorn the outer wall surfaces. The monastery has a rich library of old ecclesiastical books and manuscripts, and the museum contains heirlooms of inestimable value. From the date of its foundation to the present day, the Kykkou Monastery has engaged in intellectual, spiritual and social activity, and has made a notable contribution to the national liberation struggles of the Greek Cypriots. The first President of Cyprus, Archbishop Makarios III served in the Kykkou Monastery as a neophyte, and later became its abbot. In accordance with his wishes, he was buried after his death in 1977 at Throni, three km. from the monastery.

2nd ROUTE:
Tamasos - Macheras - Pitsilia

Our second route in the province of Nicosia will give us the opportunity to get to know the southern parts of the province. From Nicosia, we proceed to the south-west along the valley of the river Pedieos, visiting the church-catacomb of the Panayia Chrysospiliotissa, stopping at the archaeological site of Tamasos, and then ascending towards the mountains of Macheras, to visit the monastery of this name.

In the surrounding region we shall see villages with traditional architecture, before moving on to the mountain area of Pitsilia, where the inhabitants always had a hard struggle to survive. We shall stop at some of the villages, where we should on no account fail to see the Byzantine churches with their outstanding wall-paintings - true Byzantine monuments of Cyprus.

About 11 km. from Nicosia, near the village of **Deftera**, it is worth visiting the church of the Panayia Chrysospiliotissa. The church takes the form of a catacomb within a natural cave, and is dedicated to the Virgin Chrysospiliotissa. It goes back to the Early Christian period and is thought formerly to have been covered with wall-paintings, though it has suffered great damage.

The village of **Pera**, about 18 km. south-west of Nicosia, was a part of the ancient kingdom of Tamasos, lying beyond the river Pedieos as its name implies (pera means "beyond" in Greek). The village is today famous for its traditional architecture, and also has two important churches: the **church of the Archangelos Michael**, built in the 17th c., and that of the **Panayia Odigitria**, which was erected in 1882. The ancient city-kingdom of Tamasos was in this area, near the village of Politiko.

The church of the Panayia Chrysospiliotissa.

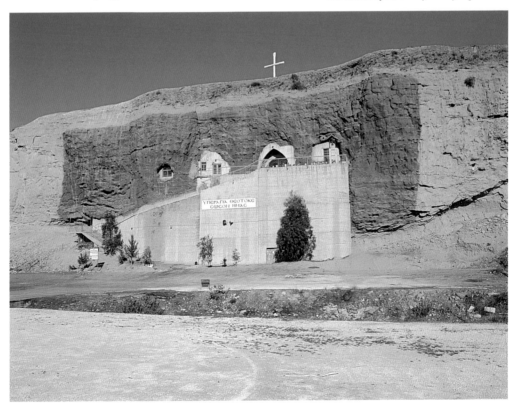

The ancient kingdom of Tamasos.

Tamasos

Tamasos was one of the twelve kingdoms of ancient Cyprus. Its economy was based on farming and the copper mines in the region, which are referred to by Strabo. The deities Aphrodite and Apollo were worshipped in Tamasos. In the surrounding area of the modern village of Politiko, tombs have been excavated or have come to light dating from the Bronze Age down to Roman times. The finds attest to the influence of the neighbouring mines on the lives of the inhabitants of Tamasos. Little is known of the kings of Tamasos, however. The mines are believed to have fallen into the hands of the Phoenicians in the 4th c. BC, and Alexander the Great later gave Tamasos to the king of Salamis, Pnytagoras, to reward him for his assistance at the battle of Tyre. Tamasos was probably an important centre in Roman times, as is clear from the Roman road that passes through it. Within the archaeological site are two royal subterranean tombs, preserved in good condition, though it is not known to which royal family they belonged.

Politiko lies on a hillside with a view in all directions. Nearby is the **monastery of Ayios Iraklidios**. Herakleidios, the son of a pagan priest, was appointed bishop of Tamasos by the apostles Paul and Barnabas. According to tradition, Herakleidios met them at Kition and took them to Paphos by way of Troodos. He was baptised in the Solia valley. He met his martyrdom at the age of 60 and was buried in the cave in which he had lived and preached the gospel. In AD 400, a church was built above his tomb, and was destroyed and rebuilt on several occasions. Originally a three-aisled church, it was renovated in the 8th c. and the 14th-15th c. The modern buildings date from 1773, when Archbishop Chrysanthos again renovated the church and cells; the wall-paintings are of the 11th c. The monastery was abandoned in the middle of the 19th c. and its property rented out. It was restored in 1963 and functions as a nunnery. The skull of St. Herakleidios is kept in a silver reliquary.

View of the Monastery of Macheras.

Proceeding to the south, we come to the **Monastery of Macheras**, one of the earliest and most important monasteries on Cyprus. During the iconoclastic controversy (730-843) Cyprus did not side with those opposed to icons, and many iconophile monks therefore sought refuge on the island. Amongst those who came to the island at this time was a monk who brought with him an icon of the Virgin. He withdrew to a cave in the mountains of Macheras, where he placed the miraculous icon.

In AD 1145, two hermits from Palestine, Neophytos and Ignatios came to Cyprus. While they were staying at the Monastery of Ayios Chrysostomos on Pentadaktylos, they saw a light flickering every night on the Troodos range opposite. When they went to find the source of the light, they came to the cave, and a voice instructed them to take the knife that appeared before them, so that they could cut through the undergrowth and enter the cave. In this way, they discovered the icon. In AD 1160, the two hermits went to Constantinople and sought the assistance of the emperor Manuel Komninos to build a monastery

dedicated to the Virgin. The emperor responded favourably to their request, and the monastery was built. During the Turkish period it was a centre of education. The national martyr Archbishop Kyprianos, who was executed on 9 July 1821, was a monk here. Each year there are two major religious festivals, on August 15 and September 8. To the north of the monastery is the hideout where Grigoris Afxentios, the hero of the Cypriot liberation struggle of 1955-59, fought and met his death. On 3 March 1957, British armies surrounded Afxentios's hideout and demanded that he surrender. Grigoris refused and after 7 hours' fierce fighting, the British poured petrol over the hideout and blew it up. Afxentios was burned to death as he fought.

In the area of Macheras lie the villages of **Gourri, Lazania** and **Phikardou**, which are famous for their traditional architecture. Phikardou was declared an ancient monument and awarded the 1988 Europa Nostra prize for the superb vernacular architecture of its houses, and its notable wood-carvings dating from the 18th c.

The houses of Katsinioros and Achilleas Dimitris - some parts of which go back to the 16th c. - have recently been restored and serve as living examples of rural architecture. Taking the road that passes through Gourri, which is only 1 km. away from Phikardou, and Kalo Chorio, we come to the Nicosia-Palaichori road and head south-west towards the villages of Pilitsia. It should be noted that not all these fall within the province of Nicosia: about half the region belongs to Limassol, the neighbouring province to the south.

The area to the east of Olympos, the highest peaks of which are Madari (1612 m) and Papoutsa (1554 m), is known by the name **Pitsilia**, and contains about 40 villages. The old villages clinging to the mountain sides, or hidden away in the valleys, retain their traditional character. The surrounding hillsides and valleys are densely planted with vines, almond-trees, pistachios, chestnuts and other trees. Amongst the small traditional villages like **Alona** and **Askas**, are a number of larger ones that have resisted the trend to move to the city, including **Palaichori** and **Agros**, which are becoming tourist attractions. **Kyperounda** and **Pelendri** lie hidden in their respective valleys. Near the village of **Lagoudera** is the old **monastery of the Panayia tou Araka**, one of the most famous Byzantine monuments of Cyprus. **Palaichori** is 45 km. south of Nicosia on the Nicosia-Agros-Limassol road. On a hill near the village stands the

monument to the Mother, erected in honour of the three heroes of the 1955-59 liberation struggle, Mastis, Karaolis and Yeoryios. In addition to its traditional architecture, the village is of great interest for its Byzantine churches: the **Metamorphosis**, which dates from the 16th c. and has some of the most exquisite post-Byzantine wall-paintings on Cyprus; and the **Panayia Chrysopantanassa**, also of the 16th c., which stands near the main square of the village and also has some highly interesting wall-paintings.

Agros, 57 km. from Nicosia and 39 km. from Limassol, is the centre of the Pitisilia area. It is named after the Megalos Agros monastery at Kyzikos in Asia Minor. According to tradition, forty monks came from the monastery at Kyzikos to Cyprus towards the end of the 11th c. in search of a sacred place, and settled at Agros, where they built a monastery of the same name. In 1894, after a dispute between the inhabitants of Agros and the Bishop of Kition, the monastery was demolished and a church devoted to the **Panayia Eleousa** built in its place. Many of the icons of the Megalos Agros monastery were preserved, along with the iconostasis and altar, and were later placed in a chapel built in the grounds of the church of Eleousa. Two of these icons, that of the Virgin Agrotissa and that of the Pantokrator, are heirlooms of great value.

Monument to the Mother (fig. 1)
at the village of Palaichori (fig. 2),
and the snow-clad village of Aska (fig. 3).

The icon of the Virgin Agrotissa is one of the 70 icons painted by St. Luke the Evangelist, and one of four similar ones brought to Cyprus and presented to the monasteries of Megalos Agros, Araka, Macheras and Trooditissa.

The village of **Platanistasa** lies at a height of 1000 m., some 15 km. from Agros. It has some fine churches, the best known of which is one of the nine Byzantine churches in the Troodos region included in the UNESCO list of the World Cultural Heritage: the **church of the Stavros tou Ayiasmati**, which has some of the fullest ensembles of wall-paintings on Cyprus, dating from the second half of the 15th c. They depict the life of Christ and the life of the Virgin, the discovery of the Holy Cross, scenes from the life of Constantine the Great, and scenes from the Old Testament. The name Platanistasa is derived from the plane-trees (platania) that used to grow in the area. There are only a few plane-trees now, though there is an abundance of pines and other flora.

Lagoudera is another outstanding mountain village in the foothills of Madari, which has luxuriant vegetation and a superb natural setting. Lagoudera has become well known for the famous Byzantine church of the Panayia tou Araka, which is internationally recognised on account of its superb wall-paintings. This church, too, is included in the UNESCO list of the World Cultural Heritage. The wall-paintings date from 1192 and are executed in the style of the late Komninian period.

The architectural design of the church is a very simple one. It has the shape of a cross with a dome at the centre. The second, timber roof was placed in position in the 14th or 15th c. The iconostasis is decorated with gold leaf and dates from the 16th-17th c. Outside the church stands a majestic oak-tree, 900 or 1000 years old, which is known as the "Gouronoklado" (pig's branch).

Two nature trails begin and end at Lagoudera, for those who like nature and walking. One is the Madari trail, and the other leads to the church of the Stavros tou Ayiasmati at Platanistasa.

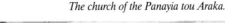

The church of the Panayia tou Araka.

3rd ROUTE:
Nisou - Pera Chorio - Dali

The third route in the province of Nicosia takes in the areas to the south and south-east of the capital.

From Nicosia we take the national highway linking Nicosia and Limassol, to explore the region known as the valley of the river Yialias. Just before the Green Line, we shall see a number of old churches, such as those of Ayios Eftychios at Nisou and the Ayioi Apostoloi at Pera Chorio; we shall also call at Dali, the site of the ancient city-kingdom of Idalion. This route may be extended to include the province and town of Larnaca, or we may return via the national highway.

Bronze plaque containing a contract between king Stasikypros and the city of Idalion and the doctor Onasilos, providing for free treatment for the wounded during the Persian siege of the city in 470 BC.

About 7 km. outside Nicosia, we turn left and come to the village of **Nisou**, just off the national highway, where it is worth visiting the little **church of Ayios Eftychios**, standing on a hill to the north-east of the village. At **Pera Chorio**, near Nisou, the **church of the Ayioi Apostoloi** is of interest both for its architecture and for its wall-paintings. It is a small, single-aisle church of the 12th c., most of the wall-paintings of which come from this same period, though there are some of later date.

Continuing to the east, we come to the village of **Dali**. This is the settlement that succeeded the ancient kingdom of Idalion, founded by Chalkanor in the 14th c. BC. In 1850, a chance find brought to light a bronze plaque bearing a long inscription in the Cypriot script. It refers to the unsuccessful siege of Idalion by the Persians and the people of Kition during the reigns of Baalmelek I, king of Kition (479-449 BC) and Stasikypros, the last king of Idalion. Since this time, the site of ancient Idalion has yielded many other Cypriot, Greek, and Phoenician inscriptions, and a large number of notable archaeological finds, the majority of which have found their way abroad and now adorn foreign museums.

To the east of the village of Dali lies **Potamia**, a Frankish fief during the Middle Ages. King Peter II had a palace here. A number of ruins attest to the wealth of this period, the chronicler of which, Leontios Macheras, states that the palace was destroyed by the Saracens in 1426. Further south, near the Attila Line, is the village of Lymbia. Its original name was probably Olympia, and it will have been a dependency of Idalion. The main church in this village was renewed in 1795, though it was probably originally built much earlier.

7

PROVINCE OF LIMASSOL

The town and routes in the surrounding area

The province of Limassol is in the south part of Cyprus. To the east it borders with the province of Larnaca, to the west with Paphos, to the north with Nicosia, and on the south it marches with the sea. The province occupies about 15% of the total area of the island, and has a population of 173,000 inhabitants, representing approximately 29% of the total population of unoccupied Cyprus. The main town and capital of the

Views of Kourion.

province is Limassol. The province of Limassol is largely mountainous or semi-mountainous, and there are narrow valleys near the coast.

Farming has long been the main occupation of the rural population. The irrigated areas are given over to citrus trees, and fruit and garden produce, while fruit-trees are grown in the semi-mountainous areas and a large region is covered by vines. Limassol is and has long been the main wine-producer of the island. The famous red wine of Cyprus is made here, the main centre being the famous wine-villages in the north of the province. In the general urban area of Limassol there are three industrial zones; the major industry is the wine-making of Limassol.

Both the town and the province of Limassol attract a large number of tourists throughout the entire year.

Our tour of the province of Limassol begins, of course, with the town of Limassol itself, which is the most important tourist and commercial centre on the island. Here, too, the old town is the most interesting part. After seeing it, we may follow three routes.

The first route leaves Limassol and heads northwest towards the southern slopes of Troodos. Passing through the picturesque villages of Alassa, Lania, Trimiklini, and Saita, we come to Platres, a famous holiday resort. Continuing towards Mount Olympos, the highest peak of Troodos, we visit Prodromos, Kyperounda, and Pelendri. Visitors may enjoy the enchanting nature trails.

The second route follows the Limassol - Paphos road to the west of Limassol and gradually takes us up to the Krasochoria.

The third route follows the old Limassol - Paphos road to villages at which there are a large number of archaeological sites, while some of them offer panoramic views and attractive beaches.

Limassol

Limassol, with about 140,000 inhabitants, is the second largest town on Cyprus. Together with the suburbs surrounding it, it is already a large town, and is continually expanding in a coastal zone about 16 km. long. It is a modern town, with fine residences, modern buildings, shops, luxury hotel complexes, countless restaurants and taverns, and entertainment places to cater for all tastes. The kernel of it is the old town, with its narrow, busy shopping streets, and old archontika ("mansions"), which are now being restored and are veritable jewels of architecture. Limassol was always famous for its conviviality, and there are many festivals and events in the town, the main ones being Carnival and the wine festival held every September. This conviviality stems from the outgoing character of the inhabitants, who have a great love of life and their town. The original name, and the precise date of the foundation of the town of Limassol are both unknown.

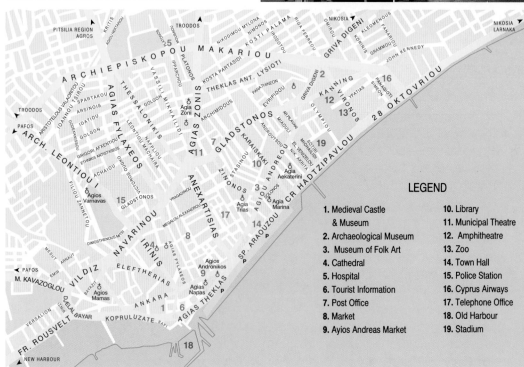

LEGEND

1. Medieval Castle & Museum	10. Library
2. Archaeological Museum	11. Municipal Theatre
3. Museum of Folk Art	12. Amphitheatre
4. Cathedral	13. Zoo
5. Hospital	14. Town Hall
6. Tourist Information	15. Police Station
7. Post Office	16. Cyprus Airways
8. Market	17. Telephone Office
9. Ayios Andreas Market	18. Old Harbour
	19. Stadium

The coast road in the town of Limassol.

Lying between the ancient kingdoms of Kourion to the west and Amathus to the east, it did not grow to any great size. During pre-Christian times it was a small anonymous settlement, the inhabitants of which were occupied mainly in stock-raising and fishing. During the Early Byzantine period, the names Neapolis and Theodosia are recorded.

After the destruction of Amathus in the 12th c., the name Neapolis came to be used. According to Constantine Porphyrogennitos in the 10th c. the town was called Nemesos, and was one of the 15 most important towns on Cyprus. The history of Limassol begins with the arrival of Richard the Lionheart of England, during the Third Crusade. In 1191, Richard celebrated his marriage to Berengaria of Navarre in the castle of Limassol. Amathus was destroyed after the defeat of Isaac Komninos's army by Richard, and Limassol embarked upon a new era. During the Frankish period, the town flourished and then entered into decline. It was the seat of a Catholic bishop until the Turkish period, after which it was afflicted by natural disasters and raids. In the Venetian period, the town was not fortified by the new rulers, and it suffered many Turkish attacks, as well as earthquakes. During the period of Turkish domination, Limassol was a wretched little village, according to the foreign travellers. The establishment of British rule marked the beginning of a steady improvement in living standards and the development of trade and industry. After the island became independent, Limassol developed both demographically and economically, and after 1974, there was explosive growth in all sectors, as the town became the most important tourist and commercial centre of Cyprus and the largest harbour on the island. A large number of foreign companies have their headquarters in Limassol.

The town of Limassol.

Tour of the town

The people of Limassol look back nostalgically to the Molos, the old sea front in the town, before it was converted into the present promenade. It is from here that our tour of Limassol will begin. The old harbour of the town was nearby. The increased needs of trade led to the construction of a new, modern harbour in the south-west of the town. A few metres to the north of the old harbour is the:

Medieval Castle of Limassol

The Castle is only a few metres away from the old harbour of Limassol, and was probably built in the 13th c. The original form of the castle is unknown, since it has suffered repeated destruction. It was restored in the 14th c. An earthquake of 1491 combined with the large number of enemy raids led to the modification of its original design. In 1191, Richard the Lionheart celebrated his marriage to Berengaria of Navarre in the castle. The Venetians later made many modifications to the castle so that is could be used in the defences of the town. The British used it as a prison. It now houses the only **Medieval Museum** on Cyprus, which contains objects dating from Early Christian times to the end of the Turkish period.

Near the medieval castle, on Ayiou Andreou Street, the old shopping centre, a few m. inside the old town of Limassol, stands the:

Church of Ayia Napa

This church was built during the Ottoman period (early 18th c.) on the ruins of an earlier Byzantine church. In 1891 it was in turn replaced by a larger structure that was completed in 1906. It is a three-aisled church with a marble iconostasis and wall-paintings, mainly on the ceiling. The icon of Ayia Napa is sheathed with silver.

1. The beach at Limassol.
2. View of the outside of the castle.
3. Exhibit from the Medieval Museum.
4. The old town of Limassol.

The Old Town of Limassol, with its old archontika ("mansions") and narrow alleys, is now a busy commercial and tourist centre, with many shops, cafes, banks and so on. In this same area, still on Ayiou Andreou Street, we come to the:

Museum of Folk Art

This is housed in a recently restored neoclassical building, and contains an extensive collection of artefacts of Cypriot folk art dating from the 19th and early 20th c. A few m. further along the same street is an imposing building that houses the:

Municipal Library of Limassol

This also serves as the cultural centre of the municipality. At the end of Ayiou Andreou Street we turn into Kaningos Square, where we find ourselves on the north side of the municipal gardens of Limassol, which offer an opportunity to take a refreshing break. In the garden is an open-air theatre, in which many events take place, mainly in the summer, and also a zoo. To the north of the garden is the:

1. *The Municipal Library.*
2, 3. *Silver cup (fig. 2) and a scarab made of agate (fig. 3), Archaeological Museum of Limassol.*
4. *The archaeological site of Amathus.*

108

Archaeological Museum of Limassol

The Museum houses a rich collection of anti-quities covering all the major periods of Cypriot history from the area of Limassol, particularly the finds from the excavations at Amathus.

Having completed our tour of the town, we take the coast road to the east, passing a large number of recreation centres, hotels, restaurants, etc., and as we leave the residential area, with the sea on our right, we come to the archaeological site of Amathus.

Amathus

Amathus was one of the ancient city-kingdoms of Cyprus and dates from the 9th c. BC. With its large harbour, it was a centre of trade until the 7th c. AD and the Arab raids. It was completely destroyed by Richard the Lionheart.

Amathus was also the centre of an important cult of Aphrodite-Astarte.

Excavations have brought to light the ruins of a temple of Aphrodite on the acropolis on the hill, the city fortifications, the ancient agora, the remains of the ancient harbour, and ruins of a Byzantine basilica and two cemeteries (to the east and west of the city). The temple of Aphrodite dates from the Roman period in the 1st c. BC. The ancient harbour of the city has been explored by a team of underwater archaeology experts, and it seems likely that it was built in the 4th c. BC, during the period of the Ptolemies.

Before the excavations began, the site was looted and some important ancient artefacts have been smuggled abroad.

1st ROUTE:

Lania - Platres - Prodromos Kyperounda - Pelendri

The first route follows the Limassol - Platres road ascending the Troodos range, where we shall get to know the southern mountain slopes, which are more readily accessible from Limassol. We shall follow the road through picturesque villages to Platres, the old resort famous throughout the Middle East. We shall ascend the highest peak of Troodos, Mount Olympos, and may choose to follow the nature trails, so as to get to know the geological history and the flora of the area.

Leaving the town of Limassol behind, we take the road that leads to the north-west, ascending the Troodos range. The hills around are almost bare.

The first village we come to is **Alassa**. This is a modern settlement built on a hill to the north of the old village, which was submerged beneath the waters of the Kourris Dam. The Kourris is a river that rises in Troodos and issues on the bay of Episkopi. Across it was built the Kourris dam, one of the largest on the island. As we proceed northwards, the landscape gradually changes and there is a superb view of the surrounding hills, strewn with tiny villages. Vines gradually begin to make an appearance.

Lania is one of the villages on our way that is worth visiting to see the traditional Cypriot architecture. The narrow paved streets, the houses with their tiled roofs and wooden door- and window-frames, and the courtyards with their flowers and large clay pithoi all make a great impression on visitors. A few km. to the north we come to **Trimiklini**, an impressive, green village with many fruit trees.

The traditional village of Lania.

Attractive scenery at Platres.

On the way we pass restaurants, cafes and open-air stalls selling the fruit produced in the region, preserves, and other Cyprus specialities. Near the road are two churches dedicated to the Panayia Eleousa. One is a modern church, and the other was built in 1744. It has a lean-to timber roof and some old portable icons. It is also worth seeing the **bridges of Trimiklini**. The old one, known as the Venetian bridge, has three asymmetrical arches and is 2.5 m. wide. It was built over the river Kourris to facilitate communications in past centuries. To the north of it is a "double bridge" built later. To the right as we ascend is the Saita dam.

After Trimiklini, some 33 km. from Limassol, we come to **Saita**, a small settlement built at a height of about 600 m. on an enchanting mountain site, and enjoying a superb view. The name of the settlement probably derives from that of a snake called the saittaris in Cyprus, though there is a view connecting it with the cult of the goddess Athena, who was known in ancient times by the epithet Saitis.

As we ascend from Saita, we come to the settlement of **Moniatis**, where the houses are hidden by the dense vegetation. As we proceed, the pines, poplars, and other forest trees gradually thicken, and the landscape becomes truly idyllic. We soon arrive at Platres. "You can't sleep at Platres for the nightingales". In this epigrammatic fashion, the Nobel-prize-winning poet Yorgos Seferis, in his poem "Eleni", encourages you to imagine and visit the place. The most famous resort on Cyprus lies hidden in greenery, its bubbling waters combining to form a wonderful natural setting. Here there are many hotels and apartments available for local and foreign tourists. Platres has long been a summer resort and a destination for famous personalities from all over the world, and it has therefore been dubbed the "Switzerland of the Mediterranean". Some very interesting excursions may be made in the surrounding areas. It is worth visiting Mesa Potamos with its waterfalls. Close by is the monastery of **Mesa Potamos**, built in the 12th c.

The *picturesque Kalidonia waterfalls*, 3.5 km. to the north of Platres, are 12 m. high, and the water falls abruptly down, forming a small lake, with the foam spreading all around. As we ascend, the road becomes narrower and more winding, and we pass through some pretty shaded archways formed by old trees - planes, pines, firs, cypresses, and thick bushes. At 1951 m. on **Olympos** or **Chionistra**, the highest peak in Troodos, there is a superb view of the bay and plain of Morphou stretching into the distance, the chromium and copper mines, and the endless forests with their picturesque tiny villages.

In winter the snow is often more than two m. deep. For those interested in winter sports, there are facilities for skiing, and also for riding, tennis, and walking along the nature trails, for those who appreciate the delights of the forest.

1. Ski centre.
2, 3. Views of the Troodos Square.
4. The Kalidonia waterfalls.

Nature trails

The nature trails make it possible to get to know the flora of Troodos, the distinctive character of which is due mainly to the particular ecological conditions deriving from the height above sea level, the rainfall, the temperatures and the geomorphology. Within an area of 4-5 sq. km. are to be found about 52% of the plants native to Cyprus. Visitors who follow the nature trails also enjoy a panoramic view in all directions. The main nature trails are: the trail of Artemis, the trail of Atalanta, the trail of the Nightingales, and the trail of Persephone.

The **trail of Artemis** is about 7 km. long. It begins at the intersection of the road to Chionistra and the Troodos-Prodromos road, and encircles Chionistra at an average height of 1850 m. It takes 2-3.5 hours to complete.

The **Trail of Atalanta**, which owes its name to Atalanta, the ancient nymph of the forests, is 9 km. long. It starts at Troodos square and ends at the settlement of Chromion, at a height of 1750 m., taking 3-5 hours to complete.

The **Trail of the Nightingales** is 2 km. long and takes 1-2 hours. It begins at the stream of Kryos Potamos near the President's summer residence, at a height of 1580 m. It follows the bank of the stream, continually crossing it, and ends at the waterfall of Kalidonia, near Platres, at a height of 1340 m. Kryos Potamos is one of the few streams that has water all the year round. The gurgling water, the varied vegetation, the dark shadows cast by the trees, and the little lakes compensate the traveller.

The **Trail of Persephone** is 3 km. long and takes 1.5 - 3 km. to complete. It begins 150 km. to the south of the Troodos square, at a height of 1720 m., and ends at a point with a superb view at 1660 m.

1. *The Monastery of the Trooditissa.*
2. *Snow-covered landscape in the Troodos.*

In the Troodos region, 5 km. north-west of Platres, we come to the **Monastery of the Trooditissa**. Tradition has it that in AD 762, during the iconoclastic controversy, a monk took refuge on Cyprus with an icon of the Virgin and settled at the monastery of Ayios Nikolaos on Akrotiri, near Limassol. After the restoration of the icons in AD 787, the Virgin appeared to the monk in a vision and told him to take the icon to a place to which he would be led by a light. The light guided the monk to a cave known as the "Cave of the Trooditissa", where he lived for the rest of his life. After his death, the lamp in the cave was lit by shepherds, hunters and woodcutters. This lamp and the icon of the Virgin led to the building of the monastery about AD 990.

The first church was a single-aisled structure with wall-paintings, which was looted and burned by the Turks in 1585, and burned down again in 1842. It has a gilded iconostasis and pulpit, and the miraculous icon of the Virgin, a work by Cornaro, was sheathed with gold and silver.

There are also some 16th c. icons revealing Italian influence. To the north of the Trooditissa we pass through some enchanting countryside and arrive at **Prodromos**. This village lies at a height of 1400 m. and has a wonderful view in many directions. The landscape is dominated by the architecture and volumes of the Hotel Berengaria, which was built in 1930 and has played its part in the tourist development of the mountain villages. Prodromos, with its natural beauty, healthy climate, and abundance of water attracts many holidaymakers in the summer, who inundate the area that lies at a height of 1570 m. between Chionistra and Prodromos, near the Prodromos dam. If we turn left at the Saita cross-roads, we can follow another circuitous route that ends, again, at Troodos square. This road takes us through the village of **Kato Amiandos** and of Karvouna. It passes through equally verdant countryside, with many fruit trees, pines, poplars and so on. The village of Kato Amiandos has long been well-known for its mines. After a twisting section of road we come to **Karvouna**. Just to the south-east of Karvouna we come to Kyperounda.

Kyperounda is a picturesque village at a height of 1100-1400 m. that is well-known for its healthy climate. It is only a few km. away from Troodos, near the villages of Platres, Kakopetria and Agros. Kyperounda is one of the largest villages in the Pitsilia region, and an ideal place for a peaceful holiday. It has a large number of churches dating from the 13th c. Further to the south, on the east of the Kourris valley, lies **Pelendri**. Set amidst lush greenery 40 km. from Limassol, this is one of the most beautiful villages on Cyprus, and has fine traditional architecture. Pelendri, too, has a well-known church, one of the nine in Troodos included in the UNESCO list of the World Cultural Heritage. This is the **church of the Timios Stavros**, a 12th c. building with icons characteristic of this period. At Pelendri there is also a **church of the Panayia Katholiki**, standing in the middle of the old village and dating from the early 16th c., which has some wall-paintings of Italo-Byzantine style.

1. *Icon from the church of the Timios Stavros.*
2. *Troodos.*

2nd ROUTE:
Omodos - Koupetra - Lophou

The second route covers the area in the north-west part of the province of Limassol, known as the Krasochoria, or "wine-villages". We shall visit some of these, such as Omodos, with its monastery of the Timios Stavros and paved square, Vasa, with its cobbled alleyways, Kilani with its painted doors and windows, Phini with its pottery, and Lophou with its stone houses. Before we come to these villages, however, we shall pass through the areas of Erimi and Sotira, where human occupation has been shown by archaeological excavation to go back to the Neolithic period.

We take the main Limassol - Paphos road and come to the village of **Erimi**, about 13 km. to the west of Limassol. Here there was an important settlement dating back to the Chalcolithic period, where the earliest copper tool on Cyprus was found. Immediately after crossing the bridge over the river Kourris, we turn right and head northwards, coming to the village of **Kandou**, where there are two old 15th c. churches, of the Chrysopolitissa and Ayia Marina. The recently restored little church of Ayia Napa, which was built in the 16th c., is situated in the Kourris valley and is also well worth visiting. Recent excavations have brought to light finds of the Neolithic period. The Neolithic settlement of **Sotira** is in this same region, about 5 km. from Kandou. The round houses are set very close together and separated only by narrow passageways. The foundations are of stone, above which the superstructure was of clay and timber, covered with mud. The settlement at Sotira was built on a hill with a water-supply close by (as there still is today), and the nearby plain provided the necessary foodstuffs. Finds from the region are on display in the Archaeological Museum at Nicosia.

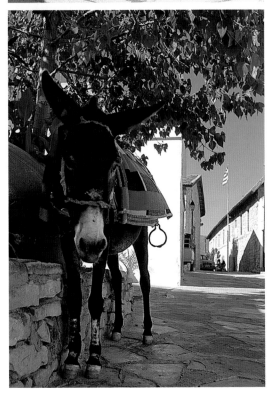

Peaceful moments in the village of Omodos.

Further along the road to Troodos, after the village of **Kybides**, the countryside becomes quite varied, and the pine-trees give way gradually to vines. This is a hilly area, with the tiny villages clinging to the hillsides, covered by the green vines in spring and summer.

We gradually move into the region known as the Krasochoria. Some of these villages are well worth visiting. This is particularly true of **Omodos** (the name of which implies a road junction in Greek), from which many roads lead to the neighbouring villages. Omodos is one of the largest Krasochoria on Cyprus, and has a famous traditional wine-press, or linos. Visitors may admire the traditional architecture of the village, with its narrow streets and stone houses, with their interior courtyards full of greenery and flowers spilling out into the alleys. In the middle of the village is the famous paved square, and the **monastery of the Timios Stavros**, which was formerly a centre of education and letters not simply for this area but for the whole of Cyprus.

According to tradition, the old village of **Koupetra** was built on the slopes of Aphamis, the mountain opposite known for its fine varieties of grapes. It was converted to Christianity about AD 150. One night the inhabitants saw a great fire on the site of the modern village of Omodos; when they searched the area, they found a small cross hidden in a cave. A little chapel was built on the site, and later a monastery, at which the many visiting pilgrims were lodged. Meanwhile, the inhabitants of Koupetra and other areas gradually transferred their homes here, creating the modern village around the monastery. The monastery has a great history. St. Helena is said to have visited it in AD 327, and left a piece of the kannabos, the hempen rope used to bind Christ's feet. This is now the most sacred heirloom of the church, and is set in a large silver cross. Another sacred heirloom, the skull of St. Philip, is kept in a silver reliquary.

The church bell dates from 1812, and was a dedication by the abbot and teacher Dositheos, who was hanged by the Turks in 1821.

The fine iconostasis of 1813 has a number of old icons, such as that of St. Philip, dating from 1628. The **three-aisled church of the Timios Stavros** stands within the two-storey monastery of considerable architectural value. It has a wood-carved ceiling and four rococo couches carved from chestnut, as well as the "throne of the Timios Stavros" with a double-headed eagle.

The monastery is no longer occupied by monks, but houses some small museums - a museum of Byzantine icons, a museum of folk art, and a museum of the liberation struggle; the last contains personal items owned by the heroes of the 1955-59 struggle against the British, a collection of historical photographs, and other objects.

Kilani is another characteristic village of this region, with impressive traditional architecture. To the west of the village is **Aphamis**, with its famous vines. An annual festival called the Aphamia is held here, which includes many cultural events. The village has two museums: the local Ecclesiastical museum, with church heirlooms dating from the 13th c. onwards, and the museum of Viticulture, where there is a display of agricultural tools connected with the growing of vines.

The **church of Ayia Mavra**, about 4 km. outside the village, was built in the 15th c. It was originally a monastery famous for its history and wall-paintings, many of which go back to the 17th c. Although these are mainly destroyed, those of St. Mavra and St. Timothy are still preserved, along with scenes from the Old and New Testament, and depictions of other saints.

Like most of the villages in this area, **Vasa** still has architecture of a traditional colour. Large clay pithoi for wine storage can be seen everywhere. At Vasa there was once a School of Byzantine Music, which was disseminated from here over the whole island.

Phini has long been famous for its pottery. The inhabitants discovered the red clay in the region, and soon turned their houses into small

pottery workshops. The characteristic pithoi in which the wine is stored are made here, along with other pots. A fine pottery museum has been built at the centre of the village, and houses a collection of vases made at Phini in past centuries.

Lophou, one of the most beautiful and historic villages on Cyprus, was built of stone in Byzantine times; its name derives from the fact that is stands on the summit of a hill (lophos) at a height of about 800 m. Its traditional architecture is largely preserved, and there is a movement to restore the houses. The cobbled streets give visitors a feeling of living in the past.

This is not the last of the Krasochoria. The entire region on the south slopes of Troodos, in the north-west part of the province of Limassol, is famous for its wine-production.

1. *Attractive view of Omodos.*
2. *Large pithoi and bunches of onions on the walls are everyday sights in the villages of Phini and Omodos.*

3rd ROUTE:

Kolossi - Kourion - Episkopi

The third route follows the old Limassol - Paphos road. As we proceed westwards, we shall see the medieval castle of Kolossi, we shall pause at Kourion to visit the archaeological site and, passing through the area of Episkopi, which belongs to the British military base, we shall have the opportunity to gaze from Pissouri over the fertile plain that stretches at its foot, or to enjoy the sea on the beautiful beaches of the area.

To the west of the town and of Lady's Mile beach, where most of the inhabitants of Limassol go to swim, we come to a zone of lush greenery, an endless Garden of the Hesperides. This is Phasouri, with its vast orchards of oranges and lemons, and its vineyards, set in geometrically laid-out plots surrounded by tall cypresses. The road passes through a natural, deeply shaded green tunnel, and the scent from the citrus trees is particularly intoxicating in the spring. This makes a pleasant, refreshing surprise before we come to the region of Kolossi.

The famous beach of Limassol.

The 7 km. we have already covered since Limassol bring us to the centre of a fertile plain, in which stands the **medieval castle of Kolossi**.

The castle was built in the 13th c. by the Lusignans, who bought the land, erected the castle, and around it created a fief, in which there were many vineyards and sugar-cane plantations. After the fall of Acre in 1291, the Knights of St. John of Jerusalem received the fief from the Lusignan king Hugo I. It swiftly became the richest estate owned by the Knights of St. John, and was known as the Grande Commanderie. The sweet wine which was, and still is, produced here, is known as Koumandaria, after the name of the fief. Interestingly, it is the oldest name of a wine in the world. In the 15th c., the governor Louis de Magnac rebuilt the castle, which is a fine example of medieval military architecture. The castle, which is in a good state of preservation, is 23 m. high, and has walls 3 m. thick. Next to it is the sugar factory, and part of the old aqueduct that supplied the latter with water can be seen to the south of the castle.

Just to the north of Kolossi we may visit the **Episkopi Museum**, at the village of the same name. The museum is a traditional two-storey building with a paved courtyard, originally designed as the private residence of the archaeologist George McFadden. It consists of two rooms, in which are displayed marble statues, tombs, amphoras, pottery, etc.

The majority of the finds are from the regions of Kourion, Kaloriziki, Ayios Ermoyenis, Phaneromeni, Episkopi, and so on, and date from the Cypro-Geometric period and Roman and Early Christian times. After visiting the museum, we move on to the ancient city-kingdom of Kourion.

1. The village of Kolossi.
2. Exhibit from the Museum at Episkopi.
3. Interior views.
4, 5. Exterior views at Kolossi.

4

5

Kourion

Built on a hill, this is one of the most impressive archaeological sites on the island, and enjoys an excellent view. Before it spreads a small, fertile plain covered with orange-trees, vines and garden produce, ending at the Akrotiri peninsula.
To right and left of it are two bays, the bay of Episkopi and the bay of Limassol.

The Akrotiri peninsula ends in a small plateau, at either side of which are the headlands of Zevgari and Kavo Gata. On the plateau stands the most important British base on Cyprus, the Akrotiri base, which has a large military airport.

Between the military base and the small plain is a salt-lake, with silvery water turned white by the salt.

The area around Kourion was probably occupied from a very early date. Nearby is the Neolithic settlement of Sotira. Herodotus records that Kourion was founded by the Argives. It is evident from the finds that it was also an important centre during the Hellenistic and Roman periods, and was destroyed by earthquakes in the 4th c. AD. It also suffered the effects of Arab raids in the 7th c. AD.
The archaeological site includes:

View of Kourion, overlooking the sea.

The Ancient Theatre

At the south of the archaeological site of Kourion is a Roman theatre, with a capacity of 3,500 spectators. It was built at the end of the 2nd c. AD and repaired in the 3rd c., before being abandoned in the 4th. Archaeological finds indicate that the theatre was built during the Hellenistic period, in the 2nd c. BC. The theatre was used for performances of ancient tragedies and comedies. In 1961, it was restored by the antiquities department and is now used for performances of plays, musical concerts, and other events.

House of Eustolios

Next to the ancient theatre of Kourion visitors may see the remains of the house of Eustolios, an imposing building of some complexity erected in the 4th c. AD. It was originally a private villa, but was converted into a public recreation centre during the Early Christian period.

The house consists of thirty rooms and baths. The floors are decorated with mosaics depicting Christian symbols such as fish, birds and geometric patterns. One inscription bears the name of Eustolios, another states that the room is adorned with figures of Aido, Sophrosyne and Eusebeia, while the largest inscription emphasises that the house is decorated with the plain symbols of Christ, and not with large stones, iron, bronze or adamant. One well-preserved mosaic depicts the head of a woman set in a circle, with the inscription Ktisis. This is the personification of Construction. In the upper part of the building, is the baths, which had frigidaria, a tepidarium and a caldarium, which had cold, luke-warm and hot water, respectively.

House of the Gladiators

The House of the Gladiators, a private residence, is named after the mosaic depicting pairs of gladiators in combat, with their names recorded in Greek, in capital letters.

House of Achilles

The House of Achilles, at the north entrance to Kourion, probably dates from the 2nd c. AD and was designed for receiving and entertaining distinguished guests. It is worth seeing the mosaic depiction of Odysseus on Skyros recognising Achilles, who was disguised as a woman. Finally, visitors to Kourion should note the remains of the drainage system, with its clay pipes, which served a town of about 30,000 inhabitants.

1, 2. View of Kourion.
3. The ancient theatre.
4. Mosaic from the House of Eustolios.
5. Mosaic from the House of the Gladiators.
6. Mosaic from the House of Achilles.

Early Christian basilica

The Early Christian basilica dates from the 5th c. AD and is one of the largest on Cyprus. It was the cathedral of Kourion and the seat of the bishop. Visitors can still see the granite columns on marble bases that separated the three aisles of the basilica. It was probably an imposing structure whose walls and floors were decorated with mosaics. To the north of the basilica is a small church, where the dedications were kept. At the entrance to it was a small rectangular cistern in which the faithful washed themselves before entering the church. The baptistery was a marble structure in the shape of a cross in the east portico of the atrium. The bishop's residence was a two-storey structure to the west of the basilica with an octagonal cistern and porticoes around the perimeter. When the buildings of Kourion were destroyed as a result of Arab raids, the bishop removed his residence far from the coast to the village that is stilled called Episkopi, which means "bishopric" in Greek.

Roman agora - Nymphaeum

Near the Early Christian basilica is a complex of buildings ranging in date from the Hellenistic period to the 7th c. AD. The Roman agora with its peristyle portico stands at the centre of the city of Kourion, and served as a meeting place for the citizens. Recent excavations have brought to light a Nymphaeum, or public spring, a complicated structure dedicated to the Nymphs, who were goddesses of natur ?.

The Stadium of Kourion

Two km. from Kourion, we come to the ancient stadium of Kourion. This was built in the 2nd c. AD during Roman times, and was used for a period of 200 years. As excavations have demonstrated, the stadium had seven rows of seats, a capacity of 6,000, and was 217 m. long and 17 wide. It was destroyed by the earthquakes of the 4th c. BC.

1. The sanctuary of Apollo Hylates.
2. The golden beach at Pissouri.

The Sanctuary of Apollo Hylates

Leaving the ancient stadium and proceeding another 2 km. along the road, we shall again stop to tour the site of the Sanctuary of Apollo Hylates. The ancient god was worshipped at Kourion as protector of forests, whence the name Hylates (hyle means "wood" or "forest" in Greek). The sanctuary dates from the 7th c. BC to the 4th c. AD, and was an important cult centre. It comprised the temple of Apollo, part of which has been restored, rooms for visiting pilgrims, a palaestra, a bath-complex, and a sacred precinct. According to Strabo, anyone who touched the altar in the sanctuary of the god Apollo was considered to have committed an act of sacrilege, and was thrown into the sea from the steep rocks in the area.

When we have finished exploring this important archaeological site, we take the road through the British base at Episkopi. As we pass through it, we can see the British settlement, and further along we may be impressed by a beautiful valley that has been converted by the British into a recreational sports area, with football grounds, cricket and hockey pitches, and so on. It has a green surface, and is set amidst steep hills, with the sea stretching before it. This area is called Happy Valley. A few km. along, the country-side changes again, and we find a green plain stretching ahead of us. It we turn off the road to the left we come to some superb sandy beaches only a few km. from the main road. Amongst the villages in this area are **Paramali, Avdimou** and **Pissouri**. The last dominates its area from a hill with a panoramic view of the plain and bay enclosed by Akrotiri Aspro. The pretty beach of the this village is the shape of a horseshoe, and the surrounding area has developed in recent years into a modern summer resort.

The main Limassol - Paphos road continues, soon leaving behind the province of Limassol and entering that of Paphos.

8

PROVINCE OF PAPHOS

The town and routes in the suttounding area

The province of Paphos is in the west part of Cyprus, and borders with the provinces of Nicosia and Limassol in the east.

The province occupies 15% of the total area of the island and has a population of about 53,000, representing approximately 9% of the total population of free Cyprus.

The capital of the

The castle of Paphos.

province is Paphos which, together with the wider urban area has a 32,500 inhabitants and is the fourth largest town in Cyprus, after Nicosia, Limassol, and Larnaca.

In the north-east of the province is part of the Troodos range, and the narrow Paphos valley stretches along the coast from Petra tou Romiou to Peyia, a distance of 45 km., though the valley is only 8 km. wide. In the north of the province is the valley of Chrysochou, which runs east and west of the town of that name. The peninsula of Akamas at the north-westernmost point of the province is a wild, uninhabited area of great interest.

The inhabitants of the province formerly worked mainly as farmers. Improvements to the irrigation system have led in recent years to considerable agricultural development, involving the growing of bananas and vines. Since 1974,

there has also been tourist development in Paphos, based on its natural beauty and rich history. It is an ideal tourist centre for those seeking to relax and explore.

We begin our tour of the province by touring the town of Paphos, in which there are many sights worth visiting, after which we may follow four routes. The first route takes the Paphos - Limassol road, and to the east of the town we come to the beautiful site of Petra tou Romiou, where the goddess Aphrodite was born.

The second route follows the coast road to the north of Paphos. We shall explore the area of Laona, ending at the picturesque fishing village of Latsi and the famous Baths of Aphrodite. Visitors have the opportunity to get to know the wonderful vegetation and greenery in the region of Akamas.

For the third route, we follow the Paphos - Chrysochou road through the valley of the river Chrysochou, to the town of the same name. From here we head east, to Pyrgos, near the confrontation line.

Finally, the fourth route visits the mountainous region of Paphos, to the west of Troodos. From here we descend to the south coast of Paphos though the Diarizos valley.

Petra tou Romiou.

Paphos

Paphos was the home and cult centre of Aphrodite Kypris, the major goddess and patron deity of the island.

According to legend, the town was founded by Paphos, son of Pygmalion and Galatea. Pygmalion made an ivory statue of a woman, which was so beautiful that he fell in love with it. Aphrodite took pity on his love and brought the statue to life. Pygmalion then married Galatea and they had a son, Paphos. Out of gratitude to Aphrodite for his parents' happiness and his own birth, Paphos founded the city that took his name, and dedicated it to her. He founded it near the place where the goddess emerged from the foaming sea, and built the first large temple to her on the summit of the neighbouring hill.

The first ancient city of Paphos was destroyed by a major earthquake, which also crushed the temple, and drained the fine harbour. New Paphos now had to be built a little further away, and a second large temple constructed. This task was carried out by Agapenor, king of Tegea and Agamemnon's admiral during the Trojan War. Some of the ruins of the first temple of Aphrodite remained at Palaipaphos (the modern village of Kouklia), however, and just beyond are the wonderful gardens of Aphrodite at Ierakipia, or Yeroskipia as it is now known. Despite all this, the archaeologist's spade has brought to light nothing earlier than the 4th c. BC. From this it has been concluded that Paphos was founded by Nikokles, one of its kings. Under the Ptolemies, in the Hellenistic period, Paphos was chosen as the capital of Cyprus, and continued to be the capital in the Roman period. In the Flavian period, it had the title of Augusta Flavia Claudia.

In AD 45 St. Paul and St. Barnabas came to Paphos, and the Roman pro-consul Sergius Paulus embraced Christianity. During the 4th c. AD, Paphos was destroyed by earthquakes. It ceased to be the capital of the island, and was replaced by Constantia, the first Christian capital of Cyprus, which was built on the ruins of ancient Salamis.

During this period the island suffered repeatedly from Arab raids, especially in the 7th c. It was at this time that the castle was built. Many of the inhabitants moved their homes inland and created the settlement of Ktima (now Pano Paphos) When Nikephoros Doukas put an end to the Arab raids in AD 965, life returned to Paphos, and in the following centuries the city flourished and prospered. In the Frankish period, it became

Evening in the harbour of Paphos.

the seat of a Catholic bishop, and under the Venetians its harbour continued to play an important role in the economy of Cyprus. During the period of Turkish domination Paphos went into decline and became an insignificant village. After the British took control of the island in 1878, however, it became a beautiful little town with metalled streets, gardens, school, churches, libraries, a law-court, and so on.

After independence, it continued to be a beautiful little town, and gradually began to play a more active role in the social, political and cultural life of Cyprus. Makarios, the first president of the Republic of Cyprus and an outstanding figure in the history of the island, came from a village in the province of Paphos.

Tour of the town

Paphos is divided into two parts: Pano Paphos, built on a hill, which is also known as Ktima, and Kato Paphos with its picturesque harbour. Visitors who take the road leading up to Pano Paphos cannot fail to be impressed by the general cleanliness and order.

Pano Paphos usually welcomes visitors with lots of flowers, whatever the season of the year. On either side of Griva Diyeni Avenue is the Municipal Library, and in front of it the Ionic "28 October" column, commemorating the Greek resistance to the Italians and the heroic epic of 1940. On the same street stand the impressive neoclassical buildings of schools like the Dimitrion primary school, the entrance to the Iakoveion Stadium, the Nikolaidion High School, and the High School of Makarios III.

Views of the town and harbour of Paphos.

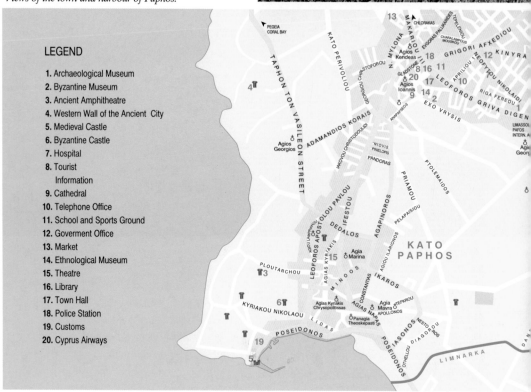

LEGEND

1. Archaeological Museum
2. Byzantine Museum
3. Ancient Amphitheatre
4. Western Wall of the Ancient City
5. Medieval Castle
6. Byzantine Castle
7. Hospital
8. Tourist Information
9. Cathedral
10. Telephone Office
11. School and Sports Ground
12. Goverment Office
13. Market
14. Ethnological Museum
15. Theatre
16. Library
17. Town Hall
18. Police Station
19. Customs
20. Cyprus Airways

Paphos.

Opposite the schools is the Paphos Town Hall and the Municipal Garden, and the bust of Kostis Palamas, and in the middle of the little Palama Square is a fountain with a dome supported on Ionic columns, with a copy of the statue of sleeping Eros in the centre. As we descend from the centre of Pano Paphos to the harbour of Kato Paphos, and along the entire sea-front, we have the opportunity to see a large number of archaeological sites, making it clear that no period of history ignored Paphos.

As we descend Apostolou Pavlou Street and turn right we come to the tourist quarter of Kato Paphos, which is at the north-west of the harbour. About 1 km. beyond this we reach the Tombs of the Kings.

Scenes from the open-air market and the small harbour of Paphos.

Tombs of the Kings

The tombs, which are also known as Palaiokastra, lie to the north-west of ancient Paphos. The site is an ancient cemetery with hundreds of subterranean burial chambers cut into the rock. The cemetery dates from the 3rd c. BC (the Ptolemaic period).

The tombs are those of private individuals, not kings: the name Royal Tombs derives from their very fine architecture. Crosses and wall-paintings in some of them indicate that in Early Christian times they probably offered refuge to persecuted Christians. The most impressive are those adorned with open peristyle courtyards with Doric columns, which are reached by steps cut into the rock and leading down to them. The entire rock face is divided into tombs of various sizes, that are cut in it.

When we have visited this site, we return by the same route and a few m. after the junction with Apostolou Pavlou Street, which connects Pano and Kato Paphos, we see on our left the:

Catacombs of Ayia Solomoni

These are cut into the rock. During the Hellenistic period and the 1st c. BC they were used as a tomb or a refuge, but were later converted into a Christian church, dedicated to St. Solomone and her seven sons. According to tradition, Solomone was pursued by Roman soldiers and took refuge in this cave, where she was buried along with her seven sons.

The catacombs are also known as the "cave of the seven sleepers". Badly damaged wall-paintings in the right part of the cave date from the 9th-12th c. BC. The attention of visitors is also attracted by **kerchiefs and pieces of cloth** tied to the tree at the entrance to the catacombs. It is said that anyone who fastens a piece of his or her clothing to the branches of the tree is cured of chronic illness.

1. *The Tombs of the Kings.*
2. *Tree at the catacombs of Ayia Solomoni.*

"Dionysos and Iokaste", mosaic from the House of Dionysos.

Mosaics of Paphos - Roman buildings

Near the harbour can be seen the finest mosaics discovered so far on Cyprus. We shall visit the House of Dionysos, the House of Theseus, the House of Aion, and the House of Orpheus. There are also some fine Roman buildings in this area, such as the Odeion, Agora and Asklepieion of Paphos.

House of Dionysos

In the years 1962-65, archaeological excavations brought to light a Roman villa decorated with the most impressive mosaics on Cyprus. It was dubbed the "House of Dionysos" because the god of wine features very frequently in the mosaics. The building covers an area of 2000 square m., of which 556 square m. are covered with mosaics. They include scenes drawn from Greek mythology, hunting scenes, and wild animals, such as tigers, wild boars, wild goats, and so on. The building consists of a peristyle courtyard at the centre, and 40 rooms. The earliest mosaic was discovered 1 m.

below the others, near the courtyard, and dates from the 3rd c. BC. It is made of small white and black pebbles and depicts Scylla, the sea-monster of the Odyssey (a combination of woman, dog and fish), holding a trident in her hand and flanked by pairs of dolphins. Of the remaining mosaics, dating from the 3rd c. AD, some have subjects drawn from Greek mythology, such as Narcissus, the four seasons, the triumph of Dionysos, Pyramos and Thisbe, Dionysos, Ikarios and Akme, Poseidon and Amymone, Apollo and Daphne, Hippolytos and Phaidra, and Ganymede.
The building was destroyed by the earthquakes of the 4th c. and never rebuilt. The archaeological site is now protected by a shelter built by the Cyprus Archaeological Service. In 1964, during the digging of the hole for a post to support the protective shelter, an amphora was discovered containing 2,484 silver coins from the Ptolemaic period (dating between 204 and 88 BC) - the largest hoard ever found on Cyprus.

House of Theseus

In 1966, the Polish archaeological mission of the University of Warsaw uncovered the Roman building known by the name of "House of Theseus", which derives from the mosaic depicting Theseus wrestling with the Minotaur. The villa lies near the harbour of Paphos, about 100 m. from the House of Dionysos. It covers an area of 9,600 square m. and was probably built in the 2nd c. AD. It was a peristyle building with a large central courtyard surrounded by a large number of rooms. The floors were decorated with mosaics. The mosaics, which cover an area of 1,400 square m., date from between the 3rd and 5th c. AD. Great interest attaches to the mosaic of Theseus, and a mosaic of Achilles. Theseus is shown killing the Minotaur, attended by the figures of Ariadne, the personification of Crete, and the Minotaur and labyrinth. In another room is a scene of the birth of Achilles, with his parents, and Anatrophe, Ambrosia and the three Fates.

House of Aion

In 1985, the Polish archaeological mission brought to light another house, known as the "House of Aion", a short distance from the House of Theseus. The house is named after Aion, god and eternal judge, who is depicted in the main mosaic floor of the house. The excavations have uncovered some superb mosaics with subjects drawn from Greek mythology, such as: "the bathing of the infant Dionysos", "Leda and the Swan," "the beauty contest between Kasiopeia and the Nereids", "the music contest between Apollo and Marsyas", and so on.

House of Orpheus

The "House of Orpheus", to the west of the House of Theseus, dates from the 3rd c. AD. Excavations have uncovered rooms with mosaic floors, amongst them an "Amazon", "Herakles" and the Nemean Lion, and "Orpheus charming the beasts".

1. The bust of Isis from the House of Theseus.
2. The mosaic of the Amazon from the House of Orpheus.

Odeion of Paphos

The Odeion, which dates from the 1st c. AD, is near the Lighthouse on the east side of a rocky hill. It was probably roofed, and was used for performances of music. In the 4th c. AD, it was destroyed by earthquake. The structure was restored in 1973. It has 11 rows of seats and houses about 1,200 people around its semicircular orchestra. The Odeion is used mainly during the summer for musical concerts and performances of drama.

Agora

In front of the Roman Odeion of Paphos are the ruins of the Agora, a large, peristyle court measuring 95 x 95 m., which dates from the 2nd c. AD.

Asklepieion

The Asklepieion, to the south of the Roman Odeion of Paphos, dates from the 2nd c. AD.

Saranda Kolones

We should not fail to visit Saranda Kolones: on a hill at the right of the main road are the remains of a Byzantine castle, probably erected in the 7th c. AD to protect the city from Arab raids. The castle is called Saranda Kolones, ("Forty Columns") after the large number of columns found in its ruins. It was destroyed by earthquake in 1222. Visitors to it may enjoy a panoramic view over the harbour of Paphos and a wonderful sunset. Also worth visiting is the **church of the Panayia Limeniotissa**, though only the ruins survive of the 5th c. Early Christian basilica dedicated to the Virgin, the patron saint of the harbour of Paphos. It is a three-aisled basilica, the aisles separated by two rows of columns. It was probably destroyed by earthquake during the 12th c. The floor had mosaics with a variety of geometric designs.

Saranda Kolones.

At the harbour of Kato Paphos, we shall visit the **Medieval Fortress of Paphos**, from where there is an excellent view over the town and the surrounding area.

The imposing fort at the entrance of the harbour of Kato Paphos immediately attracts the attention of visitors. It was originally built as a Byzantine defence-work to protect the harbour. Later, it was reconstructed by the Lusignans in the 13th c. and was then destroyed by the Venetians in 1570 during the Ottoman invasion of the island, because they were unable to defend it. The Turks rebuilt and strengthened it in 1592. In the centre of Kato Paphos, it is also worth visiting the church of **Ayia Kyriaki Chrysopolitissa** and the **Pillar of St Paul the apostle**. There is also an impressive church of the Panayia Theoskepasti.

1. *The church of Ayia Kyriaki Chrysospiliotissa.*
2. *The Frankish Baths near the church.*
3. *Icon from the Byzantine Museum.*

The church of Ayia Kyriaki Spiliotissa is in the centre of Kato Paphos. It was built in the 13th c. by the Franks in a Byzantine style with a dome, and dedicated to St Kyriaki. After the Turks conquered the island in 1571, the church was used by the Orthodox population. It is built on the mosaic floor of an Early Christian basilica dating from the 4th c.

Thirty m. to the west of the church is the marble pillar to which St. Paul is believed to have been tied and flogged when he visited Cyprus in AD 45. He is said to have been given 39 lashes by the Jews before Sergius Paulus, the governor of Cyprus, espoused Christianity. On a rock 100 m. to the east of Ayia Kyriaki stands the church of the **Panayia Theoskepasti**. During the Arab raids, a cloud is said miraculously to have covered the church, making it invisible to the raiders, leading to it being called the Panayia Theoskepasti (theoskepasti means "covered by God"). It was later destroyed by earthquake.

It was rebuilt in 1878 and is now a beautiful church with a wooden iconostasis and some valuable portable icons, and also enjoys a wonderful panoramic view.

Of the museums of Paphos, the three in the Upper Town are of particular interest. The provincial **Archaeological Museum** in Griva Diyeni Street contains a display of antiquities from the province of Paphos dating from the Neolithic period down to AD 1700.

The **Byzantine Museum**, which is housed in the Paphos Bishopric, has a notable collection of portable icons dating from the 12th to the 19th c., and other ecclesiastical objects of the Byzantine period.

Finally, the **Ethnographic Museum**, in Exo Vrysis Street, has a very extensive and interesting private collection of Cypriot folk art, including traditional furniture, agricultural implements, textiles, traditional costumes, and so on. Some of the exhibits are archaeological finds dating from the Chalcolithic period.

1st ROUTE:

Yeroskipou - Palaipaphos
Petra tou Romiou

In this first route, we shall take the Paphos - Limassol road to the east of the town. Yeroskipou, the first settlement we come to, is virtually a continuation of Pano Paphos (Ktima). This is followed by an area of plain, before we ascend to Palaipaphos, the site of the famous temple of Aphrodite in ancient times. A few km. beyond this the road brings us to Petra tou Romiou, where the goddess of love was born, according to legend.

We leave Paphos and head eastward. The region is inhabited all along the road as far as Yeroskipou. To the right and left of the road are rows of shops selling souvenirs, most of them items of Cypriot basket-weaving, and ceramics (pitchers of various sizes, ranging up to the large round pithoi that were once used to store wine). There is a museum of folk art in the village, with a display of items of traditional folk art of the last two centuries.

According to myth, **Yeroskipou** was in ancient times the sacred garden of Aphrodite, from which is took its ancient name of Hierakepia (hierakepia is the Greek for "sacred gardens"). There were forests and gardens in the area with large numbers of rare flowers and doves, the bird beloved by the goddess. The procession of the Aphrodisia passed through Hierakepia on its was to the sacred temple of the goddess at Palaipaphos. The sacred gardens and forests no longer exist, and Yeroskipou is now better known for its handicraft products, its textiles, basket-weaving, and loukoumia. The village square is dominated by the **Byzantine church of Ayia Paraskevi**. This dates from the 9th c. AD, is a domed, three-aisled basilica, with the distinctive feature of five domes forming a cross. On the south-west side of the church is a small chapel dedicated to St. Nicholas, which has some badly damaged 15th c. wall-paintings.

These depict the life and miracles of Christ, and the birth of the Virgin. One old icon of the Virgin dates from the 12th c. After Yeroskipou the road passes through the plain of Paphos which is watered by the river Ezousas. We pass by cultivated land that belongs to the villages of **Akeleia** and **Timi**. The coast at Timi is suitable for swimming and is visited by many foreigners and locals. Some 16 km. from Paphos, we ascend a hill to our left to Old Paphos, or **Palaipaphos**, and the site of the modern village of **Kouklia**. According to Pausanias, the town was founded by Agapenor of Arkadia on his way home after the Trojan War. It was the largest cult centre of Aphrodite in the ancient world. Kinyras, the king of Palaipaphos, is said to have been the first priest to serve in the goddess's temple.

1. *The church of Ayia Paraskevi at Yeroskipou.*
2. *The archaeological site at Paphos.*

Homer tells us that Kinyras sent Agamemnon, the Greek leader in the Trojan War, a bronze breastplate reinforced with gold and silver. The cult of Aphrodite was very widespread in the ancient world. Although there were many celebrations held in honour of the goddess, the most important was the Aphrodisia, which attracted people from all over Cyprus and further afield. It was held every year in spring and lasted for 4 days. The festival included sacrifices to the goddess, music, poetry and sporting competitions. From the descriptions given by poets, and from the legends that circulated in antiquity, the **temple of Aphrodite Paphia** seems to have been a majestic one. Virtually nothing of it survived when, in prehistoric times, perhaps just after the Trojan War, it was destroyed by a terrible earthquake.

Many ancient coins have a depiction of this temple on one side, with the words Koinon of the Cypriots around it. The cult of the goddess at Paphos was, in fact, so important, that the temple there evolved into a true confederacy, or koinon of the Cypriots. The centre of the temple consisted of a large, quadrangle with enormously tall, thick columns, to reach which visitors had to cross numerous courtyards and colonnades. According to legend, the centre of the temple was adorned with reliefs of outstanding art, narrating the birth, life and achievements of the goddess.

Amidst all this luxurious art, the great simplicity of the cult object, venerated by the high priests, priests and priestesses, and the thousands of worshippers who came from all parts of the known world, was naturally somewhat surprising. The statue of the goddess Aphrodite worshipped in the central quadrangle was a monolithic cone, or perhaps a pyramid.

The grottoes at Paphos hold out the promise of a unique sight well worth visiting.

This kind of likeness of Aphrodite seems to have been found in other parts of the temple, too, and in other, smaller temples nearby, for two or three of these conical monoliths are still to be found in the ruins of Palaipaphos. The gardens surrounding the temple of Aphrodite on all sides were also unique. They were planted by king Kinyras and his descendants, the Kinyrades, the priests of the temple, in order to make "her own dwelling place" as pleasing as possible to the goddess.

Rare trees and flowers were brought to Paphos to create these amazing gardens. Predominant amongst them were local flowers like the anemone, the caper, and the myrtle, which were the goddess's favourites. The dove, too, was her favourite bird. Large numbers of marble doves have been discovered in and around the temple, of which they were one of the most common forms of adornment. Today, part of the Cyclopean walls are preserved on the site, and also mosaic floors dating from Roman times. The notable finds from the excavations are kept in the **archaeological museum at Kouklia**, which is housed in the medieval palace of the Lusignans next to the ruins of the temple. The earliest remains date from the 12th c. BC. Excavation is continuing both in the sanctuary and in the ruins of the ancient city.

The feature of the site that attracts visitors' interest is, of course, the temple of Aphrodite, and the beliefs surrounding it relating to the worship of the goddess and the famous festival of the Aphrodisia, one of the most important in the ancient world. Little now remains of the original temple. A series of modifications and extensions during Roman times, together with earthquakes, have considerably altered the nature of the original structure. The medieval palace of the Lusignans, a 13th c. building next to the ruins of the ancient temple, has its own history. During the Frankish and Venetian periods it was the headquarters of a fief that included the whole of the fertile plain enclosed by the sea and the modern settlement of Kouklia. In AD 1426 it was badly damaged during a raid by the Mamelukes. Later, it was converted into a stable by the Turks.

In recent years, the south part of it has been restored. Remains of the original tower can be seen in the east section. The original square plan of the medieval building has been retained, though certain changes were made so that it could house the small Kouklia museum, in which finds from the area of Palaipaphos are displayed in chronological order.

From the hill on which this important archaeological site lies, there is a panoramic view over the sea and the surrounding plain, in which sugar cane was the main crop cultivated for five successive centuries down to the 16th c. AD. Kouklia was one of the most important sugar-producing centres in the whole of Cyprus. Recent excavations in the area have brought to light remains of windmills, which were used to supply energy to the sugar factory.

When we have seen the site at Palaipaphos, we descend again to the main Paphos - Limassol road. After a few km. the plain comes to an end, and the road, parallel with the sea in many places, brings us to the site of Petra tou Romiou. This is one of the most beautiful beaches on Cyprus. According to legend, Aphrodite, the goddess of beauty and love, was carried along by the Zephyr and emerged from the sea at this part of Cyprus. It is a little bay protected by an enormous rock, known as **Petra tou Romiou** ("Rock of the Greek") because, according to tradition, it was thrown here with superhuman strength by the Byzantine hero Diyenis Akritas to sink the ships of Arab raiders. To get a good view of the site, we may stop on the right side of the road, as it rises towards Limassol, or sit for a while in the tourist pavilion a few m. above on the side of a hill. Although the water is deep near the Rock, many are tempted to enjoy the sun and sea at this "legendary" beach.

Views of Petra tou Romiou and the grottoes.

The picturesque beach at Petra tou Romiou.

2nd ROUTE:
Coral Bay - Latsi
Baths of Aphrodite - Akamas

On this second route, we follow the coast road to the north of Paphos. Close to the town are the villages of Chlorakas, Lemba, Emba, and Kisonerga. They are followed by the Bay of Maa, better known as Coral Bay, which is ideal for swimming, Peyia, near which are the ruins of two Early Christian basilicas with fine mosaics, and Kathikas, which is half way along the Paphos - Poli road. This is followed by other villages in the area, which is known by the name Laona. Latsi, the north harbour with picturesque fish-taverns and beautiful beaches, awaits us. Close by is the place where the goddess of love used to bathe, the famous Baths of Aphrodite. This is a good place from which to get to know the north-west peninsula of Cyprus, Akamas. This area, which is uninhabited and has a virgin landscape, has many pleasant surprises to offer those prepared to explore it.

Starting from the town of Paphos, we proceed northwards, following the road through tourist complexes built in a traditional island style, and large and small hotels. Our gaze is captivated by the blue of the intricate coastline that spreads below. The villages in this area each have something special to offer.

At the village of **Emba** is the **church of the Panayia Chryseleousa**, which dates from the 12th c., and has portable icons of the 15th and 16th c. At **Lemba**, 5 km. to the north of Paphos, excavations have brought to light some important settlements of the Chalcolithic period. Visitors can see a reconstruction of the houses of that time. Further along, at the village of **Kisonerga**, there is another settlement of the Chalcolithic period which has yielded important finds. After Kisonerga, the road passes through extensive banana plantations.

Before us is the open sea. Still following the coast road, we come in a few km. to the **Bay of Maa** (also known as Coral Bay).

The archaeological site in the area of Kisonerga.

The beautiful beach at Coral Bay.

Large hotel complexes and apartments have now been erected in this area, along with shops and restaurants, to cater for the thousands of local and foreign visitors to the region.

Further north is the village of **Peyia**. About 4.5 km. outside the village, near the cape Drepanon, are the ruins of two Early Christian basilicas with fine floor mosaics. There was probably a settlement of the Early Christian period in the area. There are tombs of Roman times overlooking the sea, dug into the rock. In the paved square of Peyia are the well-known, picturesque "Peyia Springs".

The village of **Kathikas**, built of stone on the top of some low hills 22 km. from Paphos, is one of the villages on the Laona plateau. It was once a halting place for merchants and travellers, since it lies half way along the road from Paphos to Poli. Here men and animals rested at the small inn that once stood in the village. It is still a most attractive village, surrounded by vines and famous for the quality of its grapes.

In the middle of the Laona plateau is the beautiful village of **Arodes** (Kato and Pano Arodes), with an excellent view to east and west. **Kritou Tera**, a few km. beyond Arodes is a stone-built village at a height of about 470 m. The name Kritou probably derives from some person called Erotokritos in the Byzantine period, while Tera was another village, which was united with Kritou. This is a fertile region, with natural features that attract nature lovers. The Centre for Environmental Studies here conducts research into the rich natural environment of the region.

The village is also well-known for the church of the Panayia Chryseleousa (19th c.), for the Frankish-Byzantine church of Ayia Ekaterini, the old water-mill, and its abundant springs. The family of the dragoman of Cyprus, Chatziyorgakis Kornesios, who was the most powerful figure in the Greek community of Cyprus at the beginning of the 19th c., came from Kritou.

Having crossed the plateau of Laona the road descends to the bay of Chrysochou, where we come to the picturesque fishing village of **Latsi**. The small, horseshoe-shaped harbour has two lighthouses, and there is a wooden jetty 45 m. long near the middle of it. There are many good fish-taverns at Latsi, and to right and left of the small harbour are some beautiful sandy and pebble beaches. Excursions by caique are run from Latsi to Akamas, as far as Fontana Amorosa, or even further.

A few km. from Latsi we come to the site of the **Baths of Aphrodite** (Loutra tis Aphroditis), which lies between Poli and the Arnaoutis headland. The landscape here is outstanding. There is a superb view over the bay of Chrysochou, which is regarded by many as the finest view on the island. After swimming in the sea, the foam-born god-dess used to take her bath in the cool little pool, in an idyllic setting made fragrant by wild flowers. According to legend, it was here that she first met her beloved Adonis.

Adonis was hunting in the forest of Akamas when he stooped to drink water from a spring and caught sight of the naked goddess bathing in the water of the pool, each of them being dazzled by the beauty of the other.

It is said that whoever drinks water from the spring of love feels younger and is more sensitive to love (the water is not drinkable). In some legends, the goddess Aphrodite and Adonis are replaced by Rigena and Diyenis, the medieval queen and the Byzantine hero respectively. Below the Baths of Aphrodite is the *"Fontana Amorosa"*, a really beautiful area. In recent history, it served as a refuge for boats seeking shelter in the bay, or wishing to take on water. It is now an ideal swimming place. Tradition claims that the goddess Aphrodite swam here. The spring water is a few m. beneath the surface of the sea. **Ayios Nikolaos**, to the south-east of Fontana Amorosa, is a strip of land by the sea on which there are a large number of potsherds, attesting to the existence of an ancient settlement. There are still wall-paintings in the ruined church of Ayios Nikolaos. There was evidently quarrying activity in this strip of land, and there is a unique formation resembling an ancient theatre at one point.

The Baths of Aphrodite are the starting and finishing point of two trails. The "Aphrodite" nature trail takes us to the tower of the Rigena, and returns to its starting point by way of the path along the coast. The "Adonis" nature trail also takes us to the Rigena tower, but returns by way of a south route to the main Poli - baths of Aphrodite road. The total length of each trail is about 7.5 km., and the time needed to walk them ranges from 2 to 4 hours. There is a third trail called "Smigies", which ends at the starting point. These trails do not require guides, since the places of interest are sign-posted.

1, 2. The little harbour and beach at Latsi.
3. The Baths of Aphrodite.

Akamas

Akamas, the north-west peninsula of Cyprus, is a wild, uninhabited region with virgin countryside, romantic and untouched by humans. It has a great variety of characteristic features, with its vegetation, wild life, and geology, its beautiful sites and beaches, and affords real pleasure for visitors.

There are several versions of the origins of its name, one of them deriving it from Akamas, son of Theseus, who came to Cyprus after the Trojan War and founded Akamantis. The romantic sites in this area are associated with the goddess of love and Adonis. There are two other ways of reaching Akamas, in addition to the route starting from the Baths of Aphrodite: one from Ayios Yeoryios Peyias, by way of the unmetalled road along the west coast, and one from Neo Chorio, via Smigies.

Enchanting view of Akamas.

Visitors who take the former of these pass by a large sandy beach called Toxeftra or Ayios Thodoros, to the east of which a path leads to the beginning of the gorge of Avakas.

The **gorge of Avakas**, which is about 2 km. long, starts at Koloni (or Arodes) and ends at Toxeftra. To explore the gorge from Koloni, visitors walk along a deep valley enclosed by sheer rocks, rising as high as 100 m. in places. There is a unique variety of vegetation (trees and wild flowers), as well as wild animals and native and migratory birds.

Along the coast the rocks form caves, little bays, and steep recesses and projections. The flora is very rare. The unmetalled road calls at Ayioi Phanentes, where the church is preserved in ruins, before reaching the beach of Lara. This is semicircular in shape and extends for about 1.5 km. To the north of the beach there are holes, caves and hollows in the rock where the seawater penetrates and, during the summer months, evaporates, leaving behind small salt-pools. In former times, the villagers from the surrounding area used to gather salt here.

Further north is **Ammoudi** beach, shaped like a horseshoe, with small rocks at either end. There has been a turtle hatchery here since 1978. The turtles come to this isolated beach and lay their eggs in the sand, mainly during August and September. Turtle eggs from other beaches are also brought here to hatch in secure conditions.

North of Lara, visitors see enormous rocks, to which, according to tradition, the Saracens used to tie their ships before setting out on their raids in the surrounding area.

The Gorge of Avakas.

There are said to have been 101 churches in Akamas, of which only a few remains still survive. As we proceed northwards, a row of small islands come into sight to the west: Yeranisos, Kioni, Koppos and Kannoudia.

The road ends at **Kioni**, beyond which are military exercise ranges for the British forces stationed on Cyprus. A black marble column in the sea stands as a witness to an archaeological site that has not yet been investigated (possibly the point that marked the end of ancient Akamantis).

The second route starts at Neo Chorio and passes to the west of Smigies. There is a picnic area 2 km. from Neo Chorio.

At Sandalies, Stavropigi, Skotini, Pissouros and Smigies, all of them close to each other, visitors to Akamas may lose themselves in the legends surrounding Diyenis and Rigena.

At **Sandalies** their game was interrupted because they lost each other. They met again at **Stavropigi**, where there is a spring (pigi = spring).

Another time, Diyenis could not find Rigena in the darkness, and the place was therefore called **Skoteini** (skoteini = dark). On another hill, Rigena surprised Diyenis by coming up on him like a shadow, but he could not catch her because it was as dark as pitch. The hill was therefore called **Pissouros** (pissa = pitch). Finally they met and embraced at **Smigies** (smigein = meet). Proceeding northwards, we come to **Magnisia**, where magnesium was extracted and exported in the past. **Kephalovrysi** nearby is set amidst dense pine trees.

The tour ends at **Mount Sotira** near the east coast, from where there is a superb view.

On the beach of Lara there is a hatchery for sea-turtles, that protects them and helps them develop.

3rd ROUTE:
Monastery of Ayios Neophytos Chrysochou - Pyrgos

On this third route, we proceed northwards towards the interior of the province of Paphos. Some 9 km. from Paphos, to the west of the Paphos - Poli road, stands the Monastery of Ayios Neophytos, or Enkleistra. After this we continue northwards through the Valley of the river Chrysochou and descend to the town of Chrysochou. Our route continues to the east of the Bay of Chrysochou along the coast road, to the tower of Tillyria, just before the confrontation line.

Beginning at Pano Paphos (Ktima), we proceed to the north. The road ascends to the hilly area surrounding the town of Paphos on the north. The villages to the right and left of the road are gradually tending to be united with the urban zone of Pano Paphos. We shall make a diversion to the west of the main road to visit Tala and, from there, the Enkleistra, the monastery of Ayios Neophytos

Monastery of Ayios Neophytos

The monastery, 9 km. north of Paphos, was founded in 1159 by the Cypriot hermit St. Neophytos. St. Neophytos was born in 1134 at the village of Kato Drys near Lefkara. From the age of 17, he lived in the monastery of Ayios Chrysostomos in the area of Kyrenia. He visited the Holy Land and, on his return to Cyprus, came to the spot on which the monastery now stands. At the age of 25, he carved the Enkleistra with his own hands. The first cell is a small chapel of the Timios Stavros, the second is the sanctuary, and the third is the room containing the office and tomb of the saint. In 1185, he invited the church-painter Theodoros

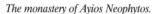

The monastery of Ayios Neophytos.

Apsevdis from Crete, who decorated the three cells with wall-paintings. These are amongst the finest wall-paintings of the Byzantine period, with full-length saints, scenes from the Passion, and representations of the Pantokrator and St. Neophytos. St. Neophytos died at the age of 85. The main church of the monastery was built 200 years later (15th c.). Despite being dedicated to the Virgin, it is known as the church of Ayios Neophytos. It is a three-aisled church in Frankish-Byzantine style, adorned with outstanding wall-paintings. St. Neophytos was one of the most important ecclesiastical writers of the 12th c.

When we have completed our visit to the monastery, we return to the main road, which continues to ascend, following a twisting route, through continually changing countryside. The road passes through densely planted almond-trees, other fruit-trees and vines. **Stroumbi** is a large village on the way, at the start of the Chrysochou valley.

The countryside continues to be green as we descend to the **town of Chrysochou**, which is referred to simply as **Poli** (Town). There are several traditions that derive the name Chrysochou from the rich, fertile valley in which it is set, or from the copper mines known to have existed in this area since ancient times, which were a major source of wealth. The region will certainly have experienced "golden" ages in antiquity.

The town is built on the site of ancient Marion, one of the city-kingdoms of Cyprus. In the Hellenistic period and later it was called Arsinoe, after the sister of Ptolemy Philadelphos. **Marion** was an important trading centre and maintained close links with Athens. It is now developing as a tourist area, since it is a picturesque town, and the surrounding area and wonderful beaches make it a memorable holiday centre.

It we continue to the east of Poli, through a coastal zone which is one of the most neglected in Cyprus, we come to Pyrgos, the last village before the Green Line. After the invasion of 1974, the proximity of the village to the confrontation

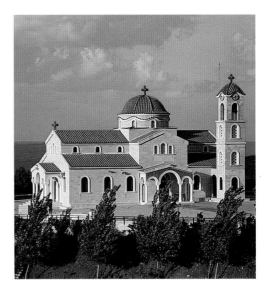

line proved an obstacle to the development in the area of tourism comparable with that of other parts of Cyprus. There are nevertheless some sandy and pebble beaches of outstanding beauty that attract visitors.

From the village of **Dimnata** to cape Pomos, the route follows one of the most picturesque coastal roads in Cyprus, with pine-clad mountains falling steeply to meet the dark blue of the sea. On the final section, from Pomos to Pyrgos, the coast road comes to an end at **Pachyammos**, and we have to turn inland to the village of **Kokkina**, which, like the surrounding area, is now part of the occupied territories. To the east of the headland of Pomos, as far as Pyrgos, the region belongs for administrative purposes to the province of Nicosia. This is the **area of Tillyria**, to which, since 1974, access has been easier from the Poli - Pomos - Pyrgos road. Before Pachyammos, with its virgin beach, is the **church of Ayios Raphael**, a pole of attraction for many pilgrims every year.

Above: the church of Ayios Raphael at Pachyammos.

4th ROUTE:

Polemi - Valley of the Cedars Pera Vasa - Diarizos Valley

The fourth route takes in the mountainous area of Paphos, which is also the west side of the Troodos range, visiting Stavros tis Psokas, the Valley of the Cedars, the village of Pano Panayia, and the monastery of the Panayia Chrysoroyiatissa. As we descend towards the south coast of Paphos, we also pass through the Diarizos valley.

The area can be approached by taking the road to the north-east of the town of Paphos, or by way of the south coast of Paphos, following the left side of the valley of the river Xeros, or from the Kykkou Monastery, in the province of Nicosia, from which we take the road to the village of Tsakistra.

There is also a fine route that starts from Pano Panayia and the monastery of the Chrysoroyiatissa and takes the road cutting across the Xeros and Diarizos rivers, by way of the medieval bridges at Roudias, Kelephos and Elia. Finally, it descends to the south coast of Paphos by way of the Diarizos valley.

To get to know the mountainous area of Paphos, we shall start from the village of **Pano Panayia**, the birthplace of Makarios III. Whatever route we take to get here, we pass through countryside of outstanding beauty.

The shortest route to the village is from Paphos, following the Paphos - Poli road to the north of Paphos, and turning right just before the village of Stroumbi. The surrounding countryside is verdant, with every inch of land given over to vines, while almonds, apples and other fruit-trees add to the beauty of the landscape.

View of Pano Panayia.

*Carefree relaxation in the
coffe-house, and the bridge of Skarfos,
following the route
for the village of Stroubi.*

The first village we come to is Polemi. The church of the Panayia Chryseleousa is a notable 13th or 14th c. monument within the boundaries of this village. **Polemi** has grown into a small agricultural town in which there are several public services. The road ascends and twists, bringing us to **Psathi** and **Ayios Dimitrianos**, two small villages built on conspicuous sites on verdant hillsides. Beyond them, we descend to **Kannavi**, a picturesque little village set amidst trees on the left bank of the river Ezousas. The road passes through shady areas where little cafes to the right and left of it invite us to take a refreshing break. The mountain mass of Troodos rises majestically before us, giving the impression that these regions are cut off from the rest of Cyprus. As we ascend, we enjoy the surrounding countryside, watching it change and become wilder and more imposing. Passing through the village of Asproyia, the road twists and turns as it ascends until we reach the village of **Pano Panayia**.

At Pano Panayia a sign directs us to the family home of Makarios III, which has been converted into a small museum. 1.5 km. away, opposite Pano Panayia, on the sides of Mount Royia, we come to the historic monastery of the Panayia Chrysoroyiatissa. The route from the south coast of Paphos to Pano Panayia is also impressive. This starts from the village of Timi and takes us by way of Axylou, Pendalia, and other villages, offering an outstanding view over the valley of the river Xeros. From Pano Panayia we may continue to the valley of the Cedars. This is an isolated valley in which the trees are predominantly cedars. It can also be reached from the Kykkou Monastery, by taking the road to the village of Tsakistra.

Cedars are amongst the most beautiful forest trees, with their dark green needles, symmetrical branches and aromatic wood. In the valley of the Cedars, they are densely planted (there are about 50,000 very tall old cedars), and their branches interlock, giving the impression of a gigantic umbrella. This is the home of the agrino, the mountain sheep of Cyprus. If we are lucky, we may see one, though it will be startled and run away. We may admire these beautiful wild animals at close quarters at Stavros tis Psokas, a large forest station, where there is a fenced area in which they are kept and protected.

Stavros tis Psokas is a large forest station. It can be reached a) from the village of Lysos to the right of the valley of Chrysochou; b) from Pano Panayia, via the valley of the Cedars; or c) from Agnia. To follow the last route we take the Kakavi-Panayia road and turn left, to follow a road that is metalled for 2 km. and unmetalled for another 7, which brings us to the picnic area of Agnia. After this we continue northwards. Although the distances seem to be small on the map, considerable time is needed to cross these isolated forest regions, since the roads are all narrow, unmetalled, forest roads that twist and turn, and may have unexpected surprises in store. Travellers are certainly rewarded for making the effort, however.

At Stavros tis Psokas there are small houses with lean-to timber roofs, at which visitors can stay. There is also an organised picnic area. The area is very cool, and is ideal in the hot summers of Cyprus.

We shall also visit some fine areas of virgin land if we choose to start from Pano Panayia and the monastery of the Chrysoroyiatissa and take a route that cuts across the Xeros and Diarizos rivers by way of the medieval bridges of Roudias, Kelephos and Elia. This is a memorable route through abandoned Turkish villages and pine forests. After the Chrysoroyiatissa Monastery we proceed to the south. First we come to **Ayia Moni**, a historic monastery built, according to tradition, in the 4th c., on the ruins of a sanctuary of Hera. In former days, a large number of monks lived here. An inscription in the left side of the entrance to the monastery informs us that it was renovated in 1696. It is now a nunnery. The road now descends and passes through two abandoned villages with destroyed houses. The 1953 earthquakes and later landslips led to the abandonment of these villages; a new village was founded a little further up, with the double name of Statos-Ayios Photios, as recently as 1974. After this, the road leads to an elevation, after which a different landscape and a panoramic view open up before us. To the left is the valley of the river Xeros, with green mountain slopes, and in the distance can be seen the Troodos range and the hills that belong to the province of Limassol. If we take the road to Pendalia, Axylos, and so on, we come to the south coast of Paphos. If we turn left, we soon come to two tiny traditional villages, **Galataria** and **Kilinia**, beyond which the metalled road comes to an end and an unmetalled road descends through green mountain slopes to **Vretsia**, a deserted Turkish village where most of the houses are now in ruins. The road passes through the "haunted village". Further down, the greenery becomes denser, and we enter the forest proper.

We continue to descend steadily until we come to the **Roudias Bridge**, which crosses the Xeros river. We are heading for Pera Vasa, which is only 14 km. from Vretsia, though the unmetalled road we are taking makes the journey seem longer. At **Pera Vasa** is an organised picnic area, and also the well-known tree of Pera Vasa, the largest pine to be found on Cyprus. It is protected and has been declared a natural monument.

From here we may proceed northwards to Milouri and beyond this to Kykkos. If we go straight on, we come to the **Kelephos (Tzelephos) Bridge**. This is 2.5 m. wide, and its arch has a span of 10.7 m. It was built over the river Diarizos and the countryside around it is superb. Further east is the **Elia Bridge**, the third of the medieval bridges. This is 2.4 m. wide and has an arch spanning 5.5 m. It is built over a tributary of the Diarizos to the west of the village of Phini. To complete the circle in this eastern part of the province of Paphos, we descend to the south coast by way of the **Diarizos valley**. This is a route followed by many travellers wishing to go from Platres-Troodos to Paphos or vice versa, because it is quite short and picturesque. All the villages we encounter on the main road, as well as those further away from it, are very pretty, and most of them are surrounded by lush greenery. Just before the Paphos-Limassol coast road, we come to Nikoklia and the Asprokremmo dam.

1. *Attractive scenery at Pera Vasa.*
2. *Wild natural countryside at the river Diarizos.*

9

PROVINCE OF LARNACA
The town and routes in the surrounding area

Exotic scenery at Larnaca.

The province of Larnaca, together with that of Limassol and part of the province of Famagusta, is in the southern part of Cyprus. It occupies about 12% of the total area of the island, and has a population of some 100,000, representing 17% of the total population of unoccupied Cyprus.

The larger part of the province of Larnaca consists of plain. In addition to corn, improvements in the irrigation system in recent years have led to the cultivaᵗ on here of garden produce and citrus fruit.

Fishing has made significant advances, with the growth of fish farms all along the coast (e.g. at Xylophagos, Ormidia, Dekelia, Larnaca, Zygi and Vasiliko). There are industrial zones in the area of Aradippou, near the harbour and the oil refinery of Larnaca. Tourism has developed in leaps and bounds, and the main tourist zones are in the town of Larnaca, on the bay of Larnaca as far as Pyla beach, and, finally, south of the international airport of Larnaca, at Kiti, Perivolia and Mazotos. Our tour begins with the beautiful town of Larnaca and the famous area of Phinikoudes, after which, we shall follow two routes.

The first route takes the Larnaca - Limassol highway to the west of the province. The first notable sight on it is the salt-lake of Larnaca. Beyond this we shall visit the villages of Kiti and Stavrovouni, and the Stavrovouni monastery. A diversion from the main road brings us to Lefkara, the village famous for its lace. We shall also, of course, visit the archaeological sites of Chirokitia and Tenda. For the second route we follow the road to the east of Larnaca and pass through an area of tourist development to Dekelia and the Kokkinochoria, a region that is part of unoccupied Cyprus.

Alley at Lefkara.

Larnaca

Larnaca is the third largest town on Cyprus, and is successor to the ancient city of Kition. The Achaeans colonised the city in the 13th c. BC, and the Phoenicians founded a strong kingdom here in the 9th c., which continued down to 312 BC, the beginning of the Ptolemaic period. The philosopher Zeno, who founded the Stoic School of philosophy in Athens, was born at Kition in 334 BC. In the 1st c. AD, the city became the second home of Lazarus, the friend of Christ, who, after being raised from the dead in Bethany, was persecuted by the Jews and fled to Kition, where he was appointed first bishop of Kition by St. Paul and St. Barnabas.

After the harbour of Kition silted up, a new city was created a mile away from the coast. It flourished down to the Roman period and went into decline when the Arab raids began (7th-10th c.).

When Cyprus was freed of the Arab threat, a site on the coast gradually came to be inhabited and called Skala.

During the Frankish period, Skala became known as Alykes, or Alyki, after the salt-lake a short distance away. The exporting of salt brought significant revenue to the town, which gradually became a trade centre at which many foreign merchants and consuls settled. In the chronicles, Skala is referred to as the town of the consulates (kousoulata).

Under the Venetian occupation, very few building works were carried out in the town. The Venetian were more interested in exploiting the natural resources of the region, and the Turks were able to capture it easily in 1570.

In the period of Turkish domination, the town retained its character as a trade and diplomatic centre. The name Larnaca was probably first used in the early years of this period, and

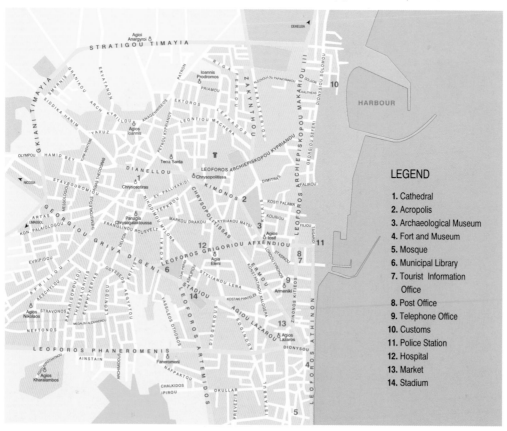

LEGEND

1. Cathedral
2. Acropolis
3. Archaeological Museum
4. Fort and Museum
5. Mosque
6. Municipal Library
7. Tourist Information Office
8. Post Office
9. Telephone Office
10. Customs
11. Police Station
12. Hospital
13. Market
14. Stadium

derives from the discovery in the area of a large number of sarcophagi (larnakes).

Under the British, the consulates were transferred to Nicosia and trading activity in the harbour declined as a consequence of the expansion of the harbours of Famagusta and Limassol. In recent years, particularly since 1974, Larnaca has seen significant economic progress. It is the home of the international airport of Cyprus, a modern harbour, the only oil refinery on the island, a marina with a capacity of 200 yachts, and a tourist zone to the east, with many modern hotels and apartments.

1. Main street in Larnaca.
2. View of the town by night.

Tour of the town

The tour of the town of Larnaca begins at the town jetty, known by the name of **Phinikoudes**. A row of tall palm-trees form a green partition and cast their protective shade on those strolling along the now busy road along the sea-front.

For many years these trees were not yet tall, and it is from this time that the name Phinikoudes ('little palm-trees') derives. A bust of Kimon, the Athenian general who was killed at Kition in a naval battle fought against the Persians in defence of the island, stood for many years on the sea-front. The municipality of Larnaca has recently redesigned this characteristic street, converting a large section into a pedestrian area, and erecting lights, islands planted with flowers, and small fountains. Cafes and restaurants are interspersed and in the summer it is a very busy area with a cosmopolitan atmosphere. On the sea-front can be seen the:

The large campanile of carved stone with relief scenes is also impressive. The exterior walls of the church incorporate grave stones engraved with the names of the notables of a bygone era. In the basement of the church, beneath the sanctuary, is a sarcophagus in which the relic of the saint was found. On it is engraved the inscription "the friend of Christ". In Zinonos Street, in the old town, we may visit the:

Pieridis Museum

This contains a fine collection of Cypriot antiquities, the product of the collecting and purchasing of ancient artefacts by five generations of the family, beginning with Dimitrios Pieridis (1811-1895). There is a display of archaeological treasures from the Chalcolithic period down to the 14th c. AD. The glass items of Roman times are of particular interest, as is the very rare medieval pottery of the 12th-14th c. In Kalogreon Square is the:

Archaeological Museum

This museum houses finds from the area dating from the Neolithic period to Roman times.

Near the Archaeological Museum, on Leontiou Machera Street, excavations have brought to light remains of the ancient city of Kition, going back to the 13th c. BC. Here visitors can see remains of the Cyclopean walls, built of enormous blocks of stone, and a complex of five temples.

As we leave the town of Larnaca on the road to Limassol, our attention is arrested by a row of 33 arches in the area of **Kamares** (kamares means "arches" in Greek). This is a stone aqueduct built in the 18th c. by the Ottoman governor of Cyprus, Bekir Pasha, to bring water to Larnaca from the Tremithos river. The stones used in its construction come from the ancient settlement of Kition.

Fort of Larnaca

The fort was originally built in the Middle Ages and received its present form in the Turkish period. The British converted it into a prison. It now houses the local Medieval Museum and in summer is used for cultural events by the Larnaca municipality. Near the fort is the Tuzla mosque, originally a three-aisled medieval church.

A few m. away from the coast, towards the centre of the town, we come to the:

Church of Ayios Lazaros

This was built in the 9th c. by the emperor Leo VI the Wise above the tomb of the saint and was renovated in the 17th c. It is one of the finest examples of Byzantine architecture on Cyprus. It is a three-aisled basilica with the aisles divided by pillars, which has decorative ancient column-capitals and the bases of three vaults in the central aisle. It has a gilded, wood-carved iconostasis of the 18th c. in baroque style with some outstanding icons.

1, 2. View of the town and the church of Ayios Lazaros.
3, 4. The Kamares (arches) and beach at Larnaca.

175

Lefkara - Chirokitia - Dekelia

In this first route, we shall take the road to the west of the international airport of Larnaca. As we proceed towards Limassol, we shall make a short diversion to visit some of the villages of the area. We shall stop at the village of Kiti to visit the church of the Panayia Angeloktisti, with its famous mosaic of the Virgin. A few km. from Kiti, towards the sea, we shall come to Perivolia and Mazotos. After this, we shall return to the main Larnaca-Limassol road and cross an extensive plain, enclosed on the left by the sea and on the right by the mountainous area of Larnaca. We shall ascend to Lefkara, a mountain village with a tradition of embroidery. We shall get to know the surrounding villages, Kato Drys, Vavla, Vavatsinia, Tochni, and Kalavasos, and we shall stop at Chirokitia and Tenda, to learn how the inhabitants of the island lived in the Neolithic period. The Larnaca salt-lakes near the international airport are the first sight one sees on arriving in Cyprus. The modern road linking the town of Larnaca with Kiti divides the lake into two.

The salt-lakes have a total area of about 3.5 square km. The bed of the lake lies two m. below sea-level. In winter, a lake of salt-water forms, which attracts many species of migratory birds, especially ducks and flamingoes, whose presence lends even greater beauty to the idyllic environment. In summer, the picture is completely different. The water evaporates, leaving a thick layer of crystalline salt covering the lake bed. The salt is of excellent quality and has been famous since the Middle Ages for its taste and whiteness; it used to be known as the salt of queen Rigena.

According to an old tradition, there were large, excellent vineyards at these salt-lakes. When St. Lazarus came to Cyprus, he disembarked a short distance from the vines. On his way to the city, he became thirsty and hungry. Seeing an old woman, he asked her for a bunch of grapes, but she refused him. In his anger, the saint cursed the vines to dry up and turn to salt. The present salt-lake is the result of the saint's curse.

Hala Sultan Tekke, a Moslem house of worship, reflected at the edge of the salt-lake.

The church of the Panayia Angeloktisti at the village of Kiti.

At the edge of the salt-lake stands a Moslem house of worship known as the **Hala Sultan Tekke**. It is dedicated to Hala Sultan or to Umm Haram, Mohammed's aunt, who died at this spot when she fell from a mule during the Arab raids of AD 649 against Kition.

The shrine, hidden amidst tall palms and other trees, is regarded as the third most holy place of pilgrimage for Moslems after Mecca and Medina.

Continuing along the road, we come to the village of **Kiti**, 12 km. from Larnaca. The village stands in the plain, and its most notable sight is the **church of the Panayia Angeloktisti**, dedicated to the Virgin. The name Angeloktisti is owed to the fact that, according to tradition, it was built by angels in a single night. An 11th c. Byzantine church, its foundations rest on the ruins of an Early Christian basilica of which all that survives is one apse, with a superb mosaic.

This has a life-size representation of the Panayia Odigitria holding the Christ child on her left arm. She is flanked by the archangels Michael and Gabriel, who have peacock's wings. The entire composition is set against a gold background made of glass tesserae covered with gold leaf, and is enclosed within a decorative border of birds, animals and plants. The mosaic, which bears the inscription SAINT MARY, dates from the 5th or 6th c. and is considered the equal of the Ravenna mosaics.

To the south of the church there is a **Frankish chapel** dating from the 14th c., which belonged to the Gibelet family and has the family coat-of-arms above the entrance. It is now a small Byzantine museum. On the north side, a Byzantine chapel of Saints Kosmas and Damian was built in the 13th c. and decorated with wall-paintings in the 15th c. To the east of the church is a terebinth tree

14 m. high, which is thought to be one of the oldest of these trees on the island.

A few km. further south, in the direction of cape Kiti, is the village of **Perivolia**. One of the characteristic sights of this village is its **Venetian tower**, a structure 8 m. high that stands 500 m. from the sea, near the lighthouse. It is divided into two storeys by a wooden floor, and has only a single opening - a rectangular window facing north.

To the west, towards cape Petounda, a dirt road parallel with the sea brings us to Petounda, where there is a spectacular view to the southeast and south-west. The site is on the borders of the village of Mazotos, where the long beach and the peaceful, idyllic setting captivate visitors.

After this, we return to the main Larnaca - Limassol road and cross an extensive plain in which corn is grown; in spring this is very green, in contrast with summer, when it changes its aspect. On our right, we see the monastery of Stavrovouni.

Stavrovouni Monastery

This is one of the earliest monasteries on Cyprus. According to tradition, it was built by St. Helena, when she put in at Cyprus on her way home from the Holy Land, to wait for the storms she had encountered at sea to subside. At night, an angel appeared to her in a dream and told her that it was God's will that she should build a church on the island, in which she should leave a piece of the Holy Cross. St. Helena awoke and asked to see the Holy Cross. To her amazement, she discovered that it was missing. Then she saw a light shining on the summit of the mountain nearby. Here, the Cross was found, and St. Helena then realised that this was the place in which she was to build the church.

The monastery of Stavrovouni,
one of the oldest monasteries in Larnaca.

An example of Cypriot architecture.

She erected a small church near Tochni and then went up to the mountain, where she built the monastery of Stavrovouni, leaving in the church a piece of the Holy Cross, the cross of the good robber, and a holy nail. The nail was lost in AD 1426, when the Egyptian general Tagriverdi destroyed the monastery church. Evidence for the cross of the good robber comes to an end in the Turkish period. All that now survives is the piece of the Holy Cross, set in a silvered Cross in the monastery church. The monastery of Stavrovouni stands on a rocky hill 750 m. high. From here, visitors can enjoy a wonderful view of the bay of Larnaca, the town of Larnaca in the distance, and the larger part of the province of Larnaca. In accordance with the strict monastic tradition, women are not allowed to enter the monastery. On 14 September, the day of the elevation of the Holy Cross, there is an impressive ceremony and celebration. In the foothills of Stavrovouni is the monastery of Ayia Varvara, where the monks have a reputation as church-painters.

Beyond this, some 40 km. from Larnaca and 8 km. from Skarinou, the road begins to ascend, twisting through hills with sparse vegetation, until it reaches Lefkara.

Lefkara is a picturesque village built on the hillside, and is named after the surrounding, white (lefkos = white), barren hills. In order to survive, the inhabitants have scattered to all corners of the earth, relying on their wits and industry to make their way. The village is famous for its embroidery. The famous Lefkaritika embroideries are exclusively made in this Cypriot village. The art is a very old one, that was probably enriched considerably under Venetian influence. When he visited Cyprus in 1481, Leonardo da Vinci is said to have commissioned a table-cloth with traditional embroidering from Lefkara for the cathedral in Milan.

Lefkara is also famous for its silverware. The village has also retained its traditional architecture, with stone houses, labyrinthine cobbled alleys, and its wooden balconies, doors, and windows. The women of Lefkara work every day on their embroidery and lace in the courtyards of their houses, which are full of flowers, or outside on the streets.

The **church of the Timios Stavros** at Ano Lefkara has a wood-carved iconostasis dating from the 18th c. According to tradition, the church replaced an earlier one built by St. Helena, which contained a piece of the Cross of Christ. At Kato Lefkara, the **church of the Archangelos Michael** has 12th and 15th c. wall-paintings. The other villages in the area include **Kato Drys**, to the south-west of Lefkara, which is the birthplace of St. Neophytos (12th c.). A restored house is said to be the saint's family home. There are several old churches in this village, the earliest of which, dedicated to the Panayia (16th c.) has recently been restored.

View from Lefkara,
with the church of the Timios Stavros.

Vavla is a small traditional village in a rich natural settling at a height of 470 m.. To the east of it is the **monastery** of **Ayios Minas**. This dates from the 15th c. and began to be used as a nunnery in 1965. The church at the centre of the monastery is a fairly plain one, but has a wood-carved iconostasis, half of which is gilded. On the north and south walls, are two large wall-paintings of St. George and St. Minas, executed in an impressive style with vivid colours. In addition to their religious duties, the nuns make religious paintings.

Vavatsinia lies to the west of Lefkara, as the road ascends to the peak of Kionia, on the southeast side of the Troodos range. It is a picturesque village on the mountainside, with traditional architecture. It is worth visiting the medieval church dedicated to the Panayia.

Tochni is a small village built of stone on two hillsides separated by a little river. Its name is probably derived from the Greek word techni ("art" or "craft") for the village was famous for its craftsmen, who carved the stone of the region with consummate skill. It still retains its traditional character, and has a very important **church of the Timios Stavros**, at the centre of the village. According to tradition, this was built by St. Helena when she visited Cyprus. The present church was rebuilt in the 19th c. on the site of the original structure, but still retains a large number of impressive features.

Near Tochni is the **archaeological site of Chirokitia**, which is certainly worth visiting, since it is thought to be the earliest settlement on Cyprus. Excavations have brought to light one of the oldest human settlements on the island, dating from 7000 BC. Built on a hill near a river, it has all the features of an advanced culture. The houses were built of stone, clay and wood and were circular in shape. The dead were buried beneath the floor in the foetal position, and were accompanied by grave offerings. All the finds from Chirokitia are now in the Archaeological Museum of Nicosia.

A few km. to the west we come to **Kalavasos**. The name of this village means "good base" in Greek, and it certainly occupied an ideal position, lying equidistantly between 3 towns (Nicosia, Larnaca and Limassol). In this area is the Neolithic settlement of Tenda which, like Chirokitia, was built on the summit of a hill, near a small river, the Vasilikos. The houses were round and made of clay or stone. The settlement was enclosed by high walls. Tenda is believed to have had about 250 inhabitants, in what was a very densely occupied area.

To the left of the national highway from Larnaca to Limassol we may visit more picturesque villages, and beaches where we can enjoy the sea and fresh fish in the fish-taverns of the area.

Taking the road to the east of Larnaca, we pass through a zone of tourist development around the bay of Larnaca with its sandy beaches. On the east side of the bay lies **Dekelia**, around which a large area belongs to the British military base. The villages beyond this are known as the **Kokkinochoria** ("red villages"), because the soil here is of a reddish colour, suitable for the growing of garden produce. It is here that the famous Cyprus potatoes are grown. We have now already entered the unoccupied area of Famagusta, and our route from here on is described in detail in the chapter devoted to this area.

Views from the archaeological site at Chirokitia.

10
PROVINCE OF FAMAGUSTA
Ayia Napa - Protaras - Paralimni
Derynia - Sotira - Frenaros - Liopetri

This area lies in the east of the island. Since very early times, both the province and the town of Famagusta have played an important role in the history of Cyprus. In recent times, from the proclamation of the independence of Cyprus in 1960 to the Turkish invasion of 1974, many factors combined to make the area the heart of the Cyprus economy. In August 1974 Famagusta was bombarded and captured by the Turks, and subsequently abandoned. Since then it has been a ghost-town.

The church of Ayioi Saranda at Cavo Greco.

The expression "unoccupied area of Famagusta" is used today to described what remains of a province that once numbered 98 settlements and now has only 9. The region was also known by the name Kokkinochoria and grew large crops of potatoes. In addition to farming and industry — industrial zones have been established at Paralimni, Derynia, Frenaro, Sotira and Avgorou — the inhabitants are mainly employed in tourism.

Tourism in the area has developed greatly, especially since 1974, and it has to some extent supplanted the occupied area as a tourist attraction. Superb beaches of fine sand, emerald sea, and an excellent hotel infrastructure have all helped to make it a pole of attraction for tourists.

Our tour of this area starts in Larnaca. Taking the road to the east, we leave behind the tourist zone encircling the bay of Larnaca. The villages after this are known as the Kokkinochoria. Our main destinations are Ayia Napa, Protaras, and Paralimni, which is the temporary administrative centre of the region. We can reach Ayia Napa either by taking the road east of Dekelia via Xylophagos, or by heading north of Dekelia along the border zone, by way of Derynia and Paralimni.

Aerial photographs of Ayia Napa.

Ayia Napa

Ayia Napa, 40 km. to the east of Larnaca, was once a small, fishing village, which had only its Venetian monastery to boast of. Since 1970, it has become a very popular summer resort. The medieval monastery is dedicated to the Virgin of the Forests (napa = forest in ancient Greek).

According to tradition, the icon of the Virgin was found in a cave. Later, the daughter of a Venetian nobleman who lived at Famagusta left her parents and came to this place, where she built a nunnery with a chapel, cells, a flour-mill, and an olive-press. Originally, it was occupied by nuns, and the chapel was a Roman Catholic church. An octagonal, domed cistern at the centre of the courtyard is carved with the figures of the Venetian lady who founded the monastery, her father and mother, and also a lion chasing a deer.

Views of the cosmopolitan resort of Ayia Napa and the little harbour.

1

In 1571, the complex became an Orthodox monastery, and was abandoned in 1773.

Today the church and the medieval monastery form an impressive monument at the centre of the village. At the east entrance is a small theatre with seats cut into the rock. On the south side of the monastery is an enormous fig-tree 600 years old. Ayia Napa is built on the slopes of a hill and spreads from the summit down to the little harbour, catering for the needs of even the most demanding visitor.

The **Museum of Marine Life** at Ayia Napa is the first of its kind in Cyprus. It houses a large collection of shells from the free areas of Cyprus, and of native and migratory birds.

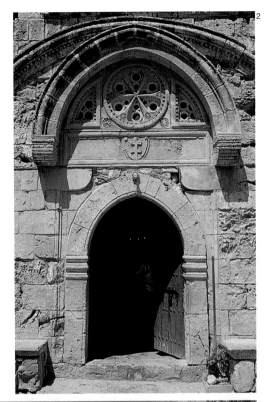

1. The beach at Ayia Napa.
2, 3. The entrance to the monastery of Ayia Napa, and view of the exterior.

The cosmopolitan holiday resort of Ayia Napa.

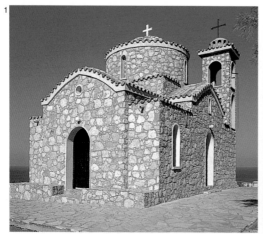

Paralimni - Protaras

After Famagusta was captured by the Turkish forces, the small town of Paralimni became the temporary administrative centre of the province of Famagusta.

Paralimni, once an insignificant village next to a lake (whence its name), has in recent years enjoyed great economic, demographic growth, and has developed as a tourist centre.

1. The church of Prophitis Ilias at Paralimni.
2. The windmills at Protaras.
3. Aerial photograph of the area of Protaras.

It has a very interesting old, two-aisled church dedicated to the Panayia. The church is decorated with unusual 18th c. porcelain plates. Parts of the church go back to the 13th c., and it houses a small Byzantine museum.

There are many other interesting churches in this area. In the Middle Ages, Paralimni was famous for its ambelopoulia - tasty little birds that formed an excellent appetiser for the gourmet.

To the east of Paralimni, **Protaras**, a famous Cypriot resort, stretches along beach 5 km. long. Golden sands, crystal clear seas, little islets, marine grottoes, rocks carved by the waves, luxury hotels and apartments, taverns serving fresh fish, and the valley of windmills, which pump water to irrigate the fruit-trees and vegetables, are all part of the landscape of Protaras.

1. Enchanting evening at Protaras.
2. Cosmopolitan beach at Protaras.
3. The grottoes at Cavo Greco.

Derynia - Sotira - Frenaros - Liopetri

A number of picturesque villages in the province of Famagusta are of particular interest for their old churches. There are three of these interesting churches at **Derynia**: Ayios Yeoryios (17th c.), Ayia Marina (15th c.) and the Panayia, which has some 17th c. icons. From here, visitors can see occupied Famagusta in the distance. At **Sotira** is the church of Ayios Mamas, originally built in the 12th c. and rebuilt in the 16th, in which some 16th c. wall-paintings are preserved. Other notable churches are those of the Panayia Chardakiotissa, about 1 km. west of Sotira, and of Ayios Yeoryios Chordakion, both of which date from the 12th c.

Frenaros, which lies at the centre of the Kokkinochoria, has some fine traditional architecture. In this village are the small Byzantine churches of Ayios Andronikos and the Archangelos Michael, which date from the 12th c. There is also an interesting 15th c. church of Ayia Marina. The village of **Liopetri**, 14 km. north-west of Ayia Napa, is famous mainly for its basket weaving. Here, too, there are some interesting medieval churches, including the Panayia Eleousa (16th c.), and the chapel of Ayios Andronikos, dating from the 15th c., which has an octagonal dome and some badly damaged wall-paintings. Near the centre of the village is the Barn of Liopetri. In 1958, after a battle with the British forces lasting many hours, four heroes of the Cyprus liberation struggle (1955-1959) were killed here. **Avgorou**, 19 km. north-west of Ayia Napa, is a country village with some interesting modern and medieval churches. To the west of the village stands the domed, free-cross church of Ayios Yeoryios Teratsiotis, which dates from the 16th c. To the north of the village, the monastery of Ayios Kendeas stands near the old Nicosia - Famagusta road. The domed church of this monastery was built in the 15th or 16th c.

The Liopetri river at Frenaros,
a meeting place for fishermen.

As we have already seen, Cyprus has been a divided island since 1974. Movement between the two parts is difficult, if not impossible. The ports and airports of unoccupied Cyprus are the official entrances to the island. The northern, occupied part of the island may be visited by foreign tourists during the daytime, from 8 a.m. to 6 p.m. It would be an omission not to describe the occupied provinces of Nicosia, Famagusta and the province of Kyrenia, including the important sights in each, and also of the region of Morphou, the ancient city of Soloi, and Vouni; this will help visitors to form a picture of these parts of Cyprus. The description begins with the occupied part of Nicosia, the cathedral of Ayia Sophia and Serayiou Square. There follows an account of historic Famagusta, with the Tower of Othello and the church of Ayios Nikolaos, which is in turn followed by a description of Enkomi, ancient Salamis, the Monastery of Apostolos Varnavas, and the church of the Panayia Kanakaria. In the province of Kyrenia, we describe the town and its castle, the Pentadaktylos range with the legendary castles of St. Hilarion, Buffavento, and Kantara, and the Abbey of Bellapais. In the same province, we note the villages of Lapithos, Karavas, Kythrea, and Myrtou. We shall become acquainted with the famous monasteries of the Apostolos Andreas, Ayios Ioannis Chrysostomos, and Ayios Panteleimon at Myrtou. Finally, we shall speak of the region of Morphou, the ancient city of Soloi, and Vouni.

CYPRUS

The ruins of ancient Salamis in occupied Famagusta, before 1974.

Famagusta

The Greek name of the town, Ammochostos, means "buried in the sand", and the city of Evagoras is renowned for its beach, which is thought to be one of the finest in the Mediterranean. The name of the first city built near modern Enkomi was Alasia. This was replaced by the well-known city of Salamis, which was destroyed by earthquake in the 4th c. AD. The city was reconstructed and given the new name of Constantia. This was in turn destroyed by Arab raids in the 7th c., and the inhabitants moved to the site of the ancient city of Arsinoe, which was "buried in the sand". From about the 10th c., this was replaced by the new town, with the name Ammochostos. During the Frankish period (1191-1571), it became one of the wealthiest and most famous cities in the world, and came to be called Famagusta (possibly meaning "having great fame"). At this time the city was enclosed within large fortification walls, which still survive and divide the old town of Famagusta from the new. In AD 1373, the city fell into the hands of the Genoese, and later those of the Venetians. In 1571, when the Turks captured Cyprus, they took Famagusta after a long siege. The inhabitants of Famagusta were driven from the town, while those who stayed behind lived in low brick houses built to the north of Famagusta. This led to the creation of a small village inhabited only by Christians. This was called varush - suburb - in Turkish, which became Varosia in Greek. This small village rapidly became one of the largest towns on Cyprus, thanks to its harbour, fertile land, and water, which was at first pumped by windmills. This led to it being called the "town of windmills". On 16 August 1974, when the Turks invaded Famagusta, the town had a population of about 40,000. Its harbour was the largest commercial port on Cyprus, and it had a well developed industry in foodstuffs, alcoholic drinks, tobacco, plastics, shoes, etc. There was also a vigorous cultural, artistic, and sporting life in Famagusta prior to 1974, and the town was adorned by some excellent cultural foundations, a Municipal Library, and a Municipal Art Gallery.

The occupied town of Famagusta, before 1974.

The monastery of Apostolos Varnavas, before 1974.

Ayios Nikolaos

The church of Ayios Nikolaos is a perfect example of Gothic architecture. Built by the Lusignans at the same period as the cathedral of Ayia Sophia in Nicosia and the monastery at Bellapais, its main aim was to impress the Cypriots and win them over to Catholicism. It is now a Turkish house of worship, called the Lala Mustafa mosque. Opposite this building are the ruins of the palace of the Lusignan kings. In the old town within the fortifications are to be found many churches, such as Ayios Yeoryios ton Ellinon, the church of the Apostoloi Petros and Pavlos, in which some wall-paintings are preserved, and Ai-Yorgis Xorinos. Another famous old church is that of the Panayia Chrysospiliotissa at Kato Varosia. There is a tradition that there were as many churches in Famagusta as there are days in the year.

The Monastery of Apostolos Varnavas

St. Barnabas was one of the most devoted of Christ's apostles. Together with St. Paul and St. Mark, he preached Christianity on the island, and later became the first bishop of Salamis. He died a martyr's death, being savagely stoned, and was buried just outside the town. His grave was discovered after a miracle, 400 years after his death. It was found by Anthemios, the archbishop of Cyprus, together with the saint's relic and a manuscript of the gospel of St. Matthew. Anthemios presented the gospel to Zeno, the emperor of Byzantium, who recognised the Cyprus church as autocephalous and bestowed various privileges on the archbishop. Anthemios later built a monastery near the grave of the saint. For many years three brothers were monks here: Stephanos, who was also abbot of the monastery, Barnabas, and Chariton. They took care of the monastery, conducted services in the church, cultivated its lands, and were fine church-painters. Hundreds of Byzantine icons came from their hands. The Turkish invaders compelled them to leave, without permitting them to take anything with them. The monastery celebrates the festival of the saint on 11 June.

Ancient Salamis

The ruins of ancient Salamis are to the east of the monastery of Apostolos Varnavas near Famagusta. Ancient Salamis was founded by a hero of the Trojan War, Teucer, brother of Ajax and son of Telamon, the ruler of the island of Salamis near Attica. Because he failed to prevent Ajax from committing suicide, his father expelled him, and he settled on Cyprus, where he founded a city-kingdom and named it Salamis, after his birthplace. Because of its geographical position and natural harbour, it was for a long time one of the most important city-kingdoms of Cyprus. For many centuries, particularly during the reign of the famous king Evagoras I, Salamis was a centre of Hellenism in the eastern Mediterranean. It was adorned by a theatre, a gymnasium, an agora, a temple of Olympian Zeus, and later by the Early Christian basilicas of St. Epiphanios and the Kambanopetra. Before the Turkish invasion in 1974, ancient tragedies were performed in the theatre.

Enkomi

The east coast of Cyprus, with its natural harbour and rich, fertile plain, was the wealthiest area of the island. A small community settled here in the 17th c. BC, and became one of the major centres on Cyprus in the Late Bronze Age, during the 14th and 13th c. The name of the new settlement was Enkomi. The archaeological site lies to the west of the modern village. From its inner harbour, copper was exported to the East and the West, and a sanctuary here has yielded a **statue of a horned** god standing on a base in the form of a copper ingot. About 1200 BC, the city was provided with "Cyclopean walls", and spacious palaces and temples were constructed of roughly dressed stone. The excavations at Enkomi have uncovered a unique urban design. Graves were found in the courtyards of some of the houses, containing a variety of objects of gold, ivory, alabaster, and bronze, as well as Mycenaean pottery with excellent decoration.

The Tower of Othello

The Tower of Othello, also known as the "citadel of Famagusta", is a square castle, with four round towers at the corners. The original building was erected in the 14th c. and had an upper storey, which was removed in 1492 by a Venetian sea-captain whose name can be seen above the main entrance to the castle, along with the winged lion of Venice. The castle is separated from the other defence-works in the town, and surrounded by a moat. The two towers at the front of it overlook the sea, and the other two the town.

A fortified jetty starting from the castle protected the harbour. The entrance to the harbour was directly opposite the castle, and could be closed by a chain. The Tower of Othello is so called because it was used by Shakespeare as the setting for his famous tragedy "Othello".

1. Sphinx, found at ancient Salamis.
2. The theatre at ancient Salamis, before 1974.
3. Statue of a horned god, from Enkomi.
4. The archaeological site of Salamis, before 1974.

The Panayia Kanakaria

The church of the Panayia Kanakaria is in the occupied village of Lythrankomi. There is a legend that an Arab who was passing by the church and saw the icon built into the outside of the lintel grew angry and shot an arrow at it. Hot blood began to flow from the Virgin's wound and fell on him. The Arab began to run towards the holy fountain to wash himself, shouting kan, which means blood in Arabic, but he was so terrified that he died. This episode led to the church being called the Panayia Kanakaria. After the Turkish invasion of the island in 1974, the church and its famous mosaics fell into the hands of the invaders. In 1979, the Turks removed the entire mosaic decoration of the apse. Many of the mosaics were destroyed during the removal, and those that survived were sold abroad.

After a successful court case instigated in New York by the Government and the Church of Cyprus, the mosaics were returned to the island in 1991 and are now on display in the Byzantine Museum of Nicosia.

Nicosia

The vicissitudes of Cyprus in recent times have left a deep mark on Nicosia, which is the last remaining divided capital in Europe. It is now a city of barbed wire, the Green Line, and culs-de-sac. The first stage in the partitioning of the capital began in 1958, with the first inter-community talks. Partition became more evident in 1963-64, when a purely Turkish-Cypriot area was created centred on the Turkish sector of Nicosia. In 1974, the area controlled by the Turks was extended and since that time the international airport of Nicosia has been in the neutral zone and is no longer used.

1. View of the exterior of the church of the Panayia Kanakaria, before 1974.

2. St. Bartholomew, mosaic from the church of the Panayia Kanakaria.

3. St. Luke, mosaic from the same church.

The medieval cathedral of Ayia Sophia

This is the largest Gothic cathedral in Cyprus. It is influenced by French architecture, particularly that of the Paris area. The construction of it began in the 12th c., and took 150 years to complete. Frankish kings were crowned and buried in it, and it was the scene of many imposing ceremonies. Since 1570, it has been a mosque. When Lala Mustafa entered the defeated city, after a siege lasting several days, he went straight to Ayia Sophia, knelt facing the direction of Mecca, and prayed to Allah. Ayia Sophia became a mosque, the Christian symbols were destroyed, and two minarets were erected that still exist today.

Serayiou Square

This is a triangular open space with an ancient column at the centre, on which, during the Venetian period, there was a stone winged lion, the symbol of the Serenissima Reppublica. After the defeat of the Venetians, the new conquerors destroyed the lion and threw out the column. The British later restored the column to its original position, and in place of the lion set a large iron cannon-ball, which had been used against the town by Lala Mustafa. Under the British regime, the column was used as a starting point from which to measure distances from the capital to other parts of the island.

From the square runs Serayiou Street, which passes in front of the Seraglio, where, in 1878, Cyprus was officially handed over to Great Britain, represented by admiral Sir John Hay, by the Turkish Kamaikam. During the Turkish period the Seraglio was an administrative centre. When the British arrived, they found the building almost in ruins. They demolished the larger part of it, built extensions, and established in it the courts, the administrative offices, the land registry, and other government services.

Until recently, there was a tree on one side of the Seraglio, on which the Turks hanged archbishop Kyprianos in 1821.

Kyrenia

The town of Kyrenia is built on an archaeological site. According to tradition, Kyrenia was founded by the Achaeans, and there are references to the kingdom of Kyrenia in historical times. The city's harbour played an important role in ancient seafaring. The Hellenistic shipwreck found off the ancient harbour, known as the "Kyrenia ship" is incontrovertible evidence for the commercial relations and trade routes of the period: Samos, Kos, Rhodes, Asia Minor coast, and Kyrenia. The bishopric of Kyrenia was instituted in the Byzantine period. There is reference to it in 1222, when it was abolished by the Franks, though it was revived in the 17th c. An Early Christian cemetery with graves cut into the rock is preserved at Chrysokava. One important monument at this site is the martyrium of Ayia Mavra, part of which is cut into the rock and the rest is built. Parts of 16th c. wall-paintings are also preserved in the martyrium. The ruins of an Early Christian basilica have been discovered at Pano Kyrenia. The Byzantine period also saw the erection of the Fort of Kyrenia. Surviving parts of the Fort date from this period, as does the octagonal Byzantine church of Ayios Yeoryios, a 10-12th c. structure. During the Frankish period, the Lusignan kings extended and reinforced the Fort, built a wall around the city, and fortified the harbour. The towers that can be seen amongst the houses of Kato Kyrenia are the remains of the city fortifications. The Venetians later improved the defences of the Kyrenia Fort, adapting it to meet the needs of the time. They demolished the royal apartments on the upper floor, opened cannon embrasures, extended the outer wall, and constructed round defence towers. After the capture of the town by the Turks in 1571, Kyrenia went into decline. In the 18th c., the Greek inhabitants of Kato Kyrenia gained their living from the sea. They had a shipyard in which they repaired and built not only fishing boats, but also caiques. Some of them were fishermen, while others traded with the Asia Minor coast and the Aegean islands. In the 19th c., some of the inhabitants of the villages in the province of Kyrenia moved to the town, where Greek sailors also settled.

Kyrenia became the administrative centre of four districts; Kyrenia, Morphou, Pentagna, and Lefka. The year 1922 was an important landmark in the life of the town. After the Asia Minor Disaster, trade with the mainland opposite declined and the harbour lost its importance. At this same period, the first hotels were built and tourism began to develop, and the 19th c. village evolved into a cosmopolitan town. As the administrative, commercial and political centre of the province, and lacking the disadvantages of the large towns, it became a pole of attraction for locals and foreigners alike, thanks to its naturally picturesque setting and good climate.

*The fort of Kyrenia
and the picturesque little harbour, before 1974.*

Kyrenia Castle

The castle is built on the east side of the harbour of Kyrenia. Its high walls are strengthened by four towers. The castle was built by Roman or Byzantine emperors, and the Franks added a variety of buildings to it to serve their own needs. The Venetians erected higher walls and towers, and made a number of modifications, giving the fortress the final form we see today.

The castle is centred on an inner courtyard, around which are living quarters, storage rooms, prisons, arsenals, and vaulted cisterns. At the entrance, a drawbridge spans the moat. In recent years, the castle courtyard has been used for various events: performances of plays, music concerts, and the festival of the flood have all been held in its evocative atmosphere. The ancient ship of Kyrenia is kept in a room specially modified for the purpose. This is a find unique throughout the entire world.

It was discovered at a depth of 33 m. in 1968-69 by a team from the University of Pennsylvania and the staff of the Cypriot Antiquities Service, under the direction of the archaeologist Vasos Karageorghis. The wreck is 14.75 m. long and 3.4 m. wide. It contained 404 amphoras full of wine, oil and almonds. These amphoras came from different pottery workshops, indicating that the ship probably took on cargo at a number of different places. Analyses have shown that the Kyrenia ship probably sank about the middle of the 3rd c. BC.

Panoramic view of the castle of Kyrenia, before 1974.

Pentadaktylos

This is the name of the mountain range in the north of Cyprus, which has been occupied by the Turks since 1974.

There are many myths and traditions relating to this range, referring not only to its wild grandeur, but also to the forts built in it. Here, conquerors fought with conquered, and Diyenis wrestled with Charon for freedom or death. One legend tells how on one occasion Diyenis was chasing the leader of the Saracens. When he saw him in the plain of Mesaoria, he placed his hand on the mountain in order to jump down into the plain. His huge fingers became imprinted there, forming the peaks of the Pentadaktylos range.

The Castle of St. Hilarion

This castle stands in the foothills of the Pentadaktylos range. It is built on a peak 725 m. high, where St. Hilarion the Great lived as a hermit in the 6th c. AD. The original fort was built by the Byzantines for defensive purposes, probably at the end of the 11th c., and was later extended by the Frankish kings. In AD 1230, it was captured by the German Emperor Frederick Barbarossa, who had taken part in the sixth Crusade, but who was expelled after two years by the Frankish ruler of Cyprus, John d'Ibelin. It was used as a base of operations against the Genoese in 1382, by the Frankish Count of Antioch, John de Lusignan. Here he killed the Bulgarian mercenaries who had helped him, tricking them and throwing them from the tower into the chasm. Ruins still survive of various parts of the castle, which was destroyed by the Venetians.

The castle of St. Hilarion, before 1974.

The castle of Kantara, before 1974.

Buffavento Castle

This castle stands on the second highest peak of Pentadaktylos, above Nicosia, at a height of 954 m. Its name is of Italian origins and means a windswept place.

The castle consists of two zones, the lower of which includes the fortification wall and towers, while the second, upper zone contains the residential quarters, the church, and the cisterns.

According to tradition, there were 101 rooms in the fort, of which one, the secret room, housed the treasures of the Rigena.

Kantara Fort

The fort is built on one of the easternmost peaks of Pentadaktylos, and is also known as the Castle of the Rigena. Like the two structures just described, it was built by the Byzantines during the 11th c. as protection against Arab raids.

The fort consists of three parts: the small bastion that protects the main entrance, the stout wall, in which is set the entrance to the castle, and the upper section with the residential rooms and cisterns. The Fort of Kantara, at a height of 630 m., is the last fort on the mountain range and controls the entrance to the Karpasia peninsula.

Abbey of Bellapais

The village of Bellapais, which spreads around the north slopes of the Pentadaktylos range, is famous for its abbey, which is an unusual example of the Gothic style in the Orient. It is built on the edge of a cliff and protected by a fortification wall and a moat on the less precipitous sides. At its centre is a peristyle courtyard with the room set around it, opening into the portico, the arches of which have engraved sculptural decoration.

The monastery has a church, a refectory, a chapter-house for meetings of the monks, dormitories, workshops, a sacristy, and a kitchen.

The refectory is highly impressive, with the coats-of-arms of the Lusignans at the entrance, the pulpit for the reading of the Holy Scriptures, and the windows offering a wonderful view over the sea and the olive groves in the plain stretching endlessly into the distance. The abbey was built and flourished during the period of the Lusignans, and was used as a summer residence by the Lusignan kings. After the end of the Frankish period, the monastery church was converted from the Catholic to Orthodox church, and was dedicated to the Panayia Asprophorousa, possibly because the Catholic monks in the abbey wore white garments.

Lapithos

Lapithos is built around the foothills of Pentadaktylos, overlooking the sea. Set amidst lavish greenery, with endless orchards of citrus trees, olives and other fruit-trees, it is watered by the Kephalovryso spring, which flows from the deep cracks in a large rock. According to tradition, Lapithos was built by Praxander, when the Achaeans colonised the area. It was one of the major ancient kingdoms of Cyprus. During the Byzantine period it was also called Lambousa ("brilliant"), reflecting the brilliance and wealth of the town.

Karavas

Like Lapithos, Karavas is built on the slopes of the mountain overlooking the sea, some 12 km. from Kyrenia. Since the 19th c., both Lapithos and Karavas have distinguished themselves in the arts and letters. Wood-carving, weaving, and embroidery flourished in the area. Karavas, too, is watered by the Kephalovryso spring. The evergreen vegetation, citrus trees, olives, and carobs, make it a very verdant place, and provide a living for the inhabitants. Before 1974, there was considerable development of tourism here, the main pole of attraction being its pretty beaches.

Kythrea

Kythrea is a large village set amidst lavish greenery about 10 km. north-east of Nicosia, on the south side of Pentadaktylos. The entire region has a very ancient history. It was the area of the ancient kingdom of Chytroi. It was here that the great saint of Cyprus, Dimtrianos, lived. The archaeological sites of the region have yielded many finds, including the famous statue of the Roman emperor Septimius Severus. The water of the Kephalovryso spring made the region of Kythrea a veritable paradise. In ancient times, this water was conveyed by an aqueduct to Salamis. In the years just before the Turkish invasion, the water was piped to thirteen villages of Mesaoria. The windmills, and the olive-presses driven by the waters of Kephalovryso once made Kythrea the "industrial" centre of the region.

Myrtou

The name Myrtou is derived from the ancient Greek word myrtos, meaning myrtle. It was first inhabited in prehistoric times, and was one of the largest villages in the province of Kyrenia. It served as the administrative centre from an early date. Down to the beginning of the 20th c., the monastery of Ayios Panteleimon was the residence of the Metropolitan of Kyrenia.

In former times, the inhabitants used to work in the marble quarries of the area, or as farmers. The larger part of the village was not irrigated, and therefore either grew wild shrubs and vegetation, or was planted with corn and carobs.

Monastery of Ayios Andreas

At the end of the Karpasia peninsula, at the north-east extremity of Cyprus, stands the famous monastery of Apostolos Andreas. The monastery has two churches: one, built in the 15th c. and revealing Gothic influence, is low down, near the source of holy water next to the sea. The later church, built in the 19th c., is higher and to the west of the first. Its large, despotic icons, by the painter Frangoulidis, include one of Saints Philon and Synesios, who lived and were active in Karpasia. Around the large monastery courtyard are set the chapterhouse, the treasury, the kitchen, the bakery, the refectories, and the hostels, at which pilgrims from all over Cyprus stayed. In the centre of the courtyard is a spring and a bust of the founder, Papa-Ioannis Ikonomou. A two-storey archbishop's residence was built in later times, together with a recreation centre for the many visitors. Down to 1974, the monastery of Apostolos Andreas was a highly popular focus for excursions throughout the entire year. It was particularly busy on 30 November and 15 August, the festivals celebrated by the monastery.

1. The monastery of Ayios Panteleimon, before 1974
2. The church of Ayios Synesios at Rizokarpaso, near Karpasia, before 1974.
3. Lapithos, before 1974.

Monastery of Ayios Panteleimon

The monastery dedicated to St. Panteleimon the Healer at Myrtou, one of the oldest monasteries on Cyprus, is one of the many shrines of the island that have been under Turkish occupation since 1974.

The present church was built about 500 years ago. It is a two-aisled, domed structure that now has no wall-paintings, since they were destroyed in 1821 by the hordes of Kutchuk Mehmet, who sacked the wealthy monastery, abused the monks, and carried off the heirlooms to Nicosia as plunder, loaded on four camels. The gilded, engraved iconostasis of the church is one of the finest on Cyprus. Made in 1743 and adorned with Byzantine icon, it is of great artistic value. It also has a large number of icons of St. Panteleimon, outstanding amongst them a large, silver-sheathed icon that was covered with pious ex votos, and an icon depicting St. Panteleimon, with Chrysanthos, the bishop of Kyrenia, kneeling at his left. This icon is associated with a renovation of the church in the year 1770. The once bustling monastery of Ayios Panteleimon is now, like the other monasteries of occupied Cyprus, silent and deserted.

Monastery of Ayios Ioannis Chrysostomos

This monastery, in the province of Kyrenia, was very prosperous and had a large number of monks, one of whom was Saint Neophytos. It was pillaged in 1571 by the Turks and abandoned by the monks. Later, it was purchased by a wealthy Christian who presented it to the Holy Sepulchre. The Monastery of Ayios Ioannis Chrysostomos. like the neighbouring monastery of Apsinthiotissa and that of Ayios Yeoryios Rigatis at Morphou, thus belongs to the Patriarchate of Jerusalem. The monastery was built in the 11th c., and has two churches, the main church of the saint and a smaller church of Ayia Triada. The main church was destroyed in the 19th c. and rebuilt. The church of Ayia Triada was built by Evmathios Philokalis, the Byzantine governor of the island, according to the founder's inscription. The Monastery of Ayios Ioannis Chrysostomos was at one and the same time an important archaeological site and a religious centre. Pilgrims from all over Cyprus used to visit it to wash in the miraculous source of holy water at the foot of a rock above the monastery.

Morphou

The west central plain is rich in history. Its passage through time is signalled by Neolithic and Bronze Age settlements, the kingdom of Soloi, and the monastery of Ayios Mamas.

Soloi, built on a privileged site in a fertile plain, rich in copper, a harbour for trade with the Orient and the Aegean, was the most important city in the region. It was preceded in the area by Aipeia, founded by the Achaeans under Demophon. The kingdom of Soloi played a leading role in the wars against the Persians in the 5th c. BC. It was besieged for five months by the Persians and destroyed during the revolt of Onesilos. After this it was placed under constant observation: the palace of Vouni was built on a neighbouring hill, from which the pro-Persian king of Marion kept watch on the people of Soloi.

The city was destroyed by a major earthquake in Roman times, after which it was rebuilt. In the Byzantine period, Soloi had its own bishop. The town was destroyed by Arab raids in the 7th c. and the inhabitants dispersed inland. The name of Soloi was a relic of the name of the area of Solea-Solia, which was part of the hinterland of the kingdom. The **church of Ayios Mamas** at Morphou was built in the early years of Christianity and destroyed by the Arabs. Two of the main centres of the region in the medieval period were Morphou and Pentagna, which were capitals of districts bearing the same names. During the period of Turkish domination, Morphou was the capital of a district that belonged for administrative purposes to the province of Kyrenia. Later, the district of Morphou was incorporated in the province of Nicosia. In 1974, the area of Morphou was one of the wealthiest and most rapidly developing parts of Cyprus. The fertile plain has the largest artesian well in the whole of Cyprus. In early modern times, there was considerable cultivation of citrus trees. Some 51% of the entire Cypriot output of citrus fruit was grown in this area. The region was also famous for its flax. The growing and processing of this crop to make thread was very difficult and required considerable knowledge and skill.

Morphou town

The name of the town comes from Morpho, an epithet of the goddess Aphrodite. This view is supported by archaeological excavations that have brought to light a sanctuary of the goddess to the north-east of Morphou. The region was inhabited from as early as the prehistoric period. One of the important monuments of the town is the monastery of Ayios Mamas, the church of which is in the Frankish-Byzantine style and dates from the early 16th c. It is built on the ruins of two Early Christian basilicas and a Byzantine church, and there is a niche in the north wall in which stands the sarcophagus of St. Mamas. The iconostasis was made in the 16th c., and is hung with icons of this same period.

The ancient city of Soloi

The ancient city of Soloi is built on a large hill commanding a very fine view over the sea and the fertile plain. Excavation of the site was suspended in 1974 and has never been resumed. The most important buildings excavated included the **theatre of Soloi** (2nd-4th c. AD), the third largest on Cyprus, after those of Salamis and Kourion; it was restored by the Cypriot department of antiquities and used for performances of ancient drama. Other buildings include: part of the Hellenistic palace, the Nymphaeum, a marble cistern with lion's heads, the basilica of Soloi, which has mosaic floors depicting dolphins, ducks, swans, and workshops of an artisan and a dyer.

Vouni

Vouni lies a short distance from Soloi, on the highest hill in the coastal mountains. A 5th c. BC palace and a temple of Athena have been discovered here. The palace is of Mycenaean type and has similarities with the palaces of Crete. It was built by king Philokypros, who is better

The monastery of Ayios Mamas, before 1974.

known as the king of Soloi, because he later built Soloi at the urging of the Athenian sage Solon, who visited him.

The ancient theatre of Soloi, before 1974.

INDEX

Bibliography

Georgiadis Klearchos «Ιστορία της Κύπρου», *Nicosia, 1978*

Karagiorgis Vasos «Αρχαία Κύπρος», *Athens, 1978*

Karouzis Giorgos «Γεωγραφία της Κύπρου», *Nicosia, 1979*

Kliridis Nearchos «Μοναστήρια στην Κύπρο», *t. b, Nicosia, 1968*
             « Θρύλοι και Παραδόσεις της Κύπρου», *Nicosia, 1954*

Michailidi M. Agni «Πάφος - Το Παλιό Κτήμα», *Nicosia, 1989*
             «Χώρα - Η Παλιά Λευκωσία», *Nicosia, 1977*
             «Το Παλιό Βαρώσι», *Nicosia, 1970*
             «Λάρνακα - Η Παλιά Σκάλα», *Nicosia, 1974*
             «Λεμεσός - Η Παλιά Πολιτεία», *Nicosia, 1981*

Chatzioannou Kyriakos «Η αρχαία Κύπρος εις τας Ελληνικά πηγάς», *Nicosia, 1971*

Encyclopaedia Chari Patsi, *Athens, 1971*

Megali Kipriaki Encyclopaedia, Editions «Φιλόκυπρος»

«Μονοπάτια της Φύσης στον Ακάμα», *Cypriot Tourist Organisation, 1994*
«Το Φυθκιώτικο Υφαντό», *Cypriot Handicrafts Service, 1995*
«Τρόοδος, Ορεινά Θέρετρα», *Cypriot Tourist Organisation, 1994*
«Πιτσιλιά», *Pitsilia Provincial Union of Migrants Associations, 1993*
«Κύπρος, 9000 χρόνια Ιστορίας και Πολιτισμού», *Cypriot Tourist Organisation, 1995*
«Η Κατεχόμενη Γη μας», *Ministry of Education, Department of Secondary Education -*
             Development Programmes Service, Nicosia, 1993